Join The Gene Pool

Join The Gene Pool

STEVEN FRANSSEN

Join The Gene Pool
Steve Franssen

First edition, 2021

Cover design: Taylor Bailey

Published by Steven Franssen

t.me/stevenfranssen

stevenfranssen.com

A diligent woman is a crown to her husband: and she that doth things worthy of confusion, is a rottenness in his bones.

Proverbs 12:4

At Home in the Saloon

I went to some alternative conservative meeting I expected would have five or six people there besides me. I was dead wrong. There were forty or fifty people. That's a big turnout for a rural area. They were all *sick and tired*. They were all *fed up*. And contrary to my experience in the past, they were quite organized. This was a change of pace. They were led by a husband and wife pair who had equal speaking time. A man came up on stage and talked about King Jesus. When a crazy person in the audience had a chance to start babbling about *The Wizard of Oz*, people cut him off pretty quickly. This is different from what it was like 15 years ago. 15 years ago, the crazies would just go on and on and nobody wanted to be unkind. Not anymore. It is hard to describe the fierce anger I encountered in others. Everyone is feeling the same way. America has been lost but America will be taken back, by God in Heaven. The globalists done hecked up, big league. The blowback for stealing what they stole is real and it is going into effect, at all levels in all jurisdictions. Americans have always loved the underdog. Now the average American is the underdog. He is a pariah in his own homeland. And the enemy is stupid and pouring in everywhere like water instead of the strategic colonization of the past. The globalists are going to get throttled, *legally*. The Swamp has been named. There is no going back. They can attempt whatever they want to attempt but people are getting it now. The globalists are going to kill a hell of a lot of people in their death throes. They won't go down easy. Especially in "enriched" areas, it's going to get ugly. The Marxists are going to be more and more astute with their raids they call "activism". Peak funding on the globalist side is not yet in sight. They still have mountains of cash to burn. But they don't have full grasp of what they're up against, either.

You just want to get people out of the cities. You want them to saddle up in outfits. That'll be what it takes. We hunt in packs. We circle the wagons. *Everybody,* of any sense, vocally wants a currency collapse. The bankers are working overtime to park all the cash they printed. The thing about thieves is that the cleverest ones will figure out something more profitable than parking it and playing the elite game. They'll cross the picket line and start an avalanche. The dam will break. Inflation will break loose. The Marxists won't get their Obama dollars anymore. They'll turn on each other. Look at that dumb broad who used all the corporate money to buy herself five mansions. You think she's going to get to keep those until the end of her days? You think she'll be able to pass that down? There's no honor among thieves. It will be taken from her by one of her own.

I enjoyed my time in the meeting place. It was a saloon with trophy mounts and Western paintings on the wall. Everybody wants to stop that development that's going in nearby. Maybe I mentioned it earlier. It's a big deal around here. Nobody wants it. California real estate developers truly are the enemy of mankind and everybody's *had it* with these lizards. You can reliably count on being questioned on your out of state license plates or phone number in most places in Montana and basically all places in Idaho outside of Boise, which is going to hell. There are places in Wyoming where you don't want to go. The Badlands are coming back. The danger is kicking up. You love to see it. What, did you think this was always going to be a cute, friendly, globally conscious *park* for you to galivant about in? No, the people who settled this land are taking it back and their blood is up. This isn't going to turn into a favela. The Federal government isn't going to get what it wants. The great mass of true Americans is on the precipice of figuring out who exactly is pulling the strings. Big trouble is setting in. Everybody's armed. Nobody's giving up their arms. The arms makers will have citizen protection and will not be shut down. Everybody around here has honky-tonk fever. Even the transplants are coming under the spell. Their inhumanity is getting hacked at like never before. It's not postcard pretty here and you can just come and eff around however you please. The old rules are setting back in. It's regional. It's demographic. Destiny is here.

America's Real History

America's was not founded on slavery. America's historical symbols are not racist. America, up until the last couple generations, was as pure a meritocracy as has been seen on the face of the Earth. The Founding Fathers were studious, accomplished Christian men who morally improved as they aged. They defeated the tyrannical banking and taxation regime of the British, who have been in a tailspin for like 250 years now, and established a system of governance morally superior to their day. This moral improvement continued with slavery being abolished in America to the tune of 600,000-800,000 white men dying in the Civil War. White men abolished slavery, not black men (or women). The slave ships weren't even run by white men. Black people owned black slaves in America.

America reached the pinnacle of its powers in the late 1800's. Everyone, of every identity group, was freer than they had ever been. Everyone had maximum economic mobility. Black people started to have real representation in government wherever they were bonafide value-creators. American innovation peaked. Everyone wore high quality clothing and medical care cost pennies. Then America joined WWI to fight for recently instituted banking interests. America killed a bunch of people off in Europe that didn't need or deserve killing and thereby shifted the balance of power to the banking society of the City of London and to the Federal Reserve system of America.

Then the banking interests rigged the stock market to fail. Corporate interests bought up the average American's depressed assets for pennies on the dollar. Black people started to lose their hard-fought standing. Famine and disease swept through the Indian communities. Franklin Delano Roosevelt lied his way into the Presidency and then lied his way into WWII by permitting Pearl Harbor to happen. Nobody wanted war in Europe again but the media egged everyone on.

America handed over nuclear secrets and uranium material, billions and billions of dollars, unending Jeeps, tanks, and planes, money printing presses, millions of pounds of food, and all sorts of other materials to Communist Russia – who used all of this to run concentration camps, genocide whoever was the target of the day, and to establish an evil permanent ruling class. FDR (through Harry Hopkins) and Churchill handed half of Europe over to Stalin at the Yalta Conference. The Soviet Union won WWII. Soviet agents poured into America, took over academia, the media, the State Department and then the intelligence agencies, and the United Nations was established on American soil. The main people capable of dissenting against this were lawyered to death, assassinated, intimidated into quiet retirement, or hounded to early graves by the media.

Communists ran America according to their interests for about 50 years. Everyone was brainwashed by advanced programming techniques developed by the CIA and other Deep State behavior modification programs. The banks kept everyone contented by stimulating artificial prosperity through money printing, consumer credit, and easy lending programs. Race relations steadily went into the gutter as everyone's freedom of association was stolen. Mass migration programs were unleashed on the public, who was never consulted for their preference. Behind closed doors, the ancient pedophilic predilections of the elite began to be fed wholesale.

The Soviet Union fell and the elite realized controlling the population through force would not work in the short to midterm and so the big switch to globalism was made. The EU was instituted. Airline travel was encouraged. V*ccinations were introduced in the media as an American Value. The millions of migrants to America had their worst inclinations toward whites stoked and inflamed. Law and order spiraled out of control. The September 11th attacks were perpetrated and then covered up, with key figures flown out of the country on military planes and other figures protected by complete and total intelligence service secrecy. The globalist American government instituted sweeping surveillance powers, instead of just doing the sensible and efficient thing of profiling radical Islamists and auditing all foreign and domestic intelligence services operating on American soil. The American people began to be openly humiliated by the regime and treated like cattle. A half-African continental, half-prostitute-born controlled-candidate was foisted upon the American people by the globalist media. You can still find a picture on the Internet of his mother putting a bottle up her vagina. He doubled and then redoubled the size of the Federal government, continued the unending wars started by the Bush Presidents, and race baited against whites every single time black people were highlighted by the media for political convenience. There started to be massive jihadi militant training compounds in rural places across America. The moneyed elite had a new bogeyman with which to divert attention away from themselves. They completely controlled "conservative" media through blackmail and bribes. Everything started to really suck and look rundown. Everyone started getting depressed and autistic. People *really* stopped reproducing. There were weird, unexplainable mass shooting events that were extremely politically convenient to the media's power. The national debt doubled and everyone started sensing that the average person was no longer seeing much, if any, of the artificial prosperity anymore.

Then a nationalist populist candidate for President named Donald Trump ran against the moneyed, anti-Christian, banking and immigration interests of the globalist's controlled-opposition (called the GOP). He promised action on the issues that really mattered to Actual Americans: immigration restriction, ending of foreign wars, protection of religious worship (with a hearty nod to Christianity), v*ccine critical thinking, restoration of race relations through economic freedom and immigration restriction, pressuring the private central bank to do right by The People, and locking up evildoers. He was allowed to win because the people controlling the vote outcome figured he was such a joke that he couldn't possibly win, and so they were neglectful in manipulating the outcome.

President Trump was somewhat successful in his agenda. He had immigration shut down by the end of his term. He ended a lot of harmful regulations and helped new infrastructure to be built. He eventually drew down troop presence in foreign theaters of war, after much farting around with the opinion of power mad generals and advisors. He helped minorities outside of his voting base get jobs and told everyone about it literally every time he spoke to the public. He pulled America out of globalist extortion agreements perpetrated under the guise of "climate change". He unleashed America's energy industry and made America energy-independent. He unified the American people in the culture war, something that was desperately needed. He broke the spell the media had over the American people by telling the truth and almost never allowing the media's verbal abuse to work on him. He quietly deprived the intelligence agencies of funding and military support. He and his wife made the White House classy again. When fraud was perpetrated against him, he told the truth to the American people – the whole way. When his life was in danger for lowering the price of pharmaceuticals and giving America favored-nation status, he subtly let the American people know. America started to feel a bit more like America again. But then the global regime released medical tyranny upon the world and President Trump got caught flat-footed.

President Trump made mistakes. He gave the pharmaceutical industry unprecedented leverage over the

American people. Ad nauseum he hired, consulted with, and endorsed people who hated his guts. He conceded critical ground in the culture war on family issues with his support of deviant sexual sins. He gave the military the shiny new weaponry and funding it would need to crush his supporters later. He gave Goldman Sachs everything it wanted. He gave foreign states everything they wanted for nothing in return. He "let bygones be bygones" with civilizational traitors (probably cause his life was credibly threatened). The world's most notorious and powerful pedophile died on his watch, just before names were going to be named. He gave leverage to fraudsters in his own ranks, who convinced him to hire dishonest, immoral judges and to burn up precious years of his tenure in wild goose chases clearing his name when his enemies never had enough votes in Congress to topple him anyway. He did not pardon civilizational heroes but chose instead to pardon drug dealers, thugs, and people who promoted imagery of his own violent death. He only declassified information that somewhat cleared his name, which was already established and cleared in the court of public opinion. He did not declassify information that would have liberated the American people. But this man's history is not yet fully written and time will tell if he rectified these and other mistakes, or not. He also inherited a situation so far gone out of control that from a historically broad perspective, his sacrifice and toil will be his prevailing legacy – if conservative Christians aren't genocided en masse and there's no one left to remember accurately.

A terrible crisis happened in the fall and winter of 2020 into early 2021. The exactly details are difficult to enumerate in published format. The globalist regime reasserted its dominance and control, began to prosecute a domestic terrorism war on conservative Christians, and every single piece of Satanic policy the globalist regime had been developing began to be unveiled to and perpetrated upon the American public. America fell yet another rung to its lowest standing ever. The descendants of America's rightful Founding Stock became an endangered species. America became a Third World tyranny in less than a month.

Rabbit Farming

There's a buck rabbit of mine who is gun shy. That is to say, he is not so good with the ladies. He lets them boss him around, throw off his advances, and bite him viciously from time to time. Every now and then he's able to somewhat mount but he just ejaculates into their backs or doesn't at all. Then he just follows them around pathetically until they are both tired and I have to take him back to his cage, bloodied and battered.

We'll call this buck Benny. I tell Benny, "Look, buddy, you have to be assertive. You can't let these girls call the shots. You have to dictate the terms and set the tone." He doesn't even look me in the eye. He cowers in his domicile. He's all hunched down and scrunched into as small a presence as possible. I says to him, "Let me see your online dating profile." We review it and he's helplessly autistic. He talks about how he watches some agitprop YouTube channel. Or he lists his favorite video games that he plays every damn day. Benny is a workaholic. He's smart. I've tested him with several metrics and determined that he's at least in the 85th percentile of intelligence. Some days he's smarter than that. Some days, usually after he's been on a porn binge or been on Tiktok too much, he's lower than that. Yet, Benny cannot help himself. He's just gun shy. He's a nice guy. He's fully convinced of consent theory. He waits for permission to do everything. He doesn't want to be in the gene pool all that much. The thing is, I need Benny to be in the gene pool. He's a decent rabbit being. He votes the right way. He eats his hay and puts on weight the right way. He has a pleasing, healthy sheen to his fur coat. He's decently sized. He's a hard worker when he wants to chew on a wood toy. I enjoy his company. He's a sweet bunny.

There's another buck rabbit of mine who is proven. He's a stud. I brought him in because Benny wasn't getting the job done. We'll call this proven buck Horace. Horace gets in there with the does and he chases em' real good and then mounts assertively. He bites them in the back of the neck and holds them there. He uses his front paws to keep his position. He does his rapid-fire thing and presto, a few weeks later there's little pink bunny babies. I've been observing Horace. He's an interesting fellow. When the snow blows through the rabbitry, he stands on top of his nesting box instead of getting in it. He lets the cold wind blow on him. He seems to like it. He takes food breaks sometimes but doesn't lose weight. He seems to tolerate hunger well. He lifts weights a few times a week. He's actually kind of a mercurial worker compared to Benny. Only does work when he feels like it but makes good coin doing it. Horace was proven from a young age. I'm told 7 months old. That's like being 18 years old in human years. Sometimes Benny and Horace play cards or talk at church but usually they are separate. They're just different creatures. Their nature is different. Horace is about as smart as Benny. Sometimes I suspect he's smarter. He knows you have to outsmart the females to get what you want.

Benny is going to have a nice long life, so long as I have a say about it. He only costs me three dollars a month in feed and water. I do want him to prove himself. We will see. I'm rooting for him. I pet him fondly on his fuzzy head. I stroke his silky ears. He is such a good rabbit. He's just gun shy. That's it, really. My neighbor demonizes Benny. He says Benny hates women. He says that Benny is a malcontent capable of extreme violence. I don't see it that way. My neighbor watches too much TV.

Bain vs. Betman

Betman went down into the tunnels beneath Gotham City. Someone had given him some clues that maybe Bain had set up his criminal enterprise down there. As Betman was creeping from shadow to shadow during his descent, a straight white male thug appeared from around the corner. He was accompanied by a straight black male thug who wore a stocking cap. Both of them had automatic machine guns, which the government doesn't allow, strapped onto their chests.

The black thug said, "Damn, it's wet as a mutha f-er down here."

"Yeah, but you shouldn't complain or Bain will conk you on the head with his fist," responded his companion. "Let's stick to our route and when our shift is over, we'll go back above ground and return to our wives and kids."

At that moment, Betman sprung from the shadows and attacked. The men did their best to raise their illegal firearms but Betman punched the white man dead with one power-assisted punch to the temple and he finished off the black man by sweeping him off his feet and then using his forearm blades in a single sawing motion to shred the black man's throat.

"I'm dying," gurgled the black man. "That's racist!"

Betman did not listen to the man's plight because he didn't believe in skin color. He stalked deeper into the heart of Bain's operations.

He came upon some men drilling into a municipal sewer shaft. Their lunches were out on a folding table. He felt hungry and so he stole a sandwich and gobbled it up as fast as he could, before anyone could notice. The sandwich went down easy. He knew he was going to need some extra energy for his fight with Bain, so he also stole a can of soda and guzzled it. He decided to spare the lives of these men because they were unarmed. They looked like city workers and Betman had a strict policy: no women and no government employees.

He stalked into a great round open area and whirled around, aghast to see unbreakable steel grates being closed behind him. He ran up to one and stared at it. Kitty Woman appeared and said, "Sorry not sorry I betrayed you. Maybe we can be boyfriend and girlfriend later?" She ran away like a cat.

"You made a serious mistake," Betman whispered, but she was already out of earshot.

Then a voice from behind him, in the center of the open area, spoke in a croaking tone, "Not as serious as yours. It's too bad you killed my men. They were cool."

"Bain!" Betman exclaimed, for it was the first time he had ever seen Bain.

"Let's not stand around and talk, Mr. *John* Betman," said Bain, using Betman's real name. "We need to fight."

"Okay," said Betman. He stalked up to Bain, who was a foot and half taller than him, nearly two hundred pounds heavier than him, and had tubes all over his body piping performance enhancing drugs into his system. Betman punched Bain hard in the face and then shoulder bumped him in the chest. Bain did not stumble even a step backwards. He lifted Betman into the air, brought Betman's body down over his thigh, and broke Betman's spine like kindling. An audible *snap* reverberated through the chamber.

"Oh, f!" howled Betman as his legs went limp. "I can't walk!"

"That's right, Betman. You should have never stood against me. Now I will take over the City of Gotham and there's nothing you can do about it."

"I am going to take a stand against you and your *socialism*, Bain."

"You're always talking about taking a stand, Betman, but I just maimed you and now you are paralyzed." His wheezing voice paused between words so he could breathe.

"You're a frickin' far right nut. You should be expelled from ever being able to call yourself a Republican." Betman tried to move his legs again but could not. "Someday I am going to stand tall and defeat you. It's just a matter of time."

"I grow weary of you, Betman. It's time for you to go away."

Bain rolled Betman's limp body into a sewage waterway. Betman howled as raw sewage filled his mouth and other orifices. His paralyzed legs got awkwardly caught on a sewer grate and he soon drowned under the rush of water, not twenty feet from where the scene of the fight played out. Bain motioned to his henchmen to fish him out of the roaring waters and they disposed of his dead body by different means.

No Consequences

There are these attractive young people living in Southern California who don't face consequences for anything they do. Mostly they smoke weed, have obscene amounts of sex, travel around and shop, and they vlog. They're given a lot of money for vlogging. Sometimes they promote products for extra money, especially the women. The women are svelte, comely, and desired by men from all over the world, especially the countries that are worker colonies for the bankers. The men are bros who go to the gym often. I watched one guy eat like a pound of edible gummies packed with pure THC. He decided that he wanted to warm up the outdoor pool by pouring pots of boiling water into it. Then he swam in the water and the video ended. Apparently, he has a stunning girlfriend he's been with since he was 15, so he's probably only having sex with her. But who knows?

These people also do podcasts. And they sleep with the prettiest porn stars. The porn stars go around America, having sex with men who write them on Instagram. They make hundreds of thousands of dollars doing this. They also have OnlyFans accounts where they do "premium porn" at prices far higher than the porn studios of yesteryear were paying. For these gorgeous young people living in California, a lot of the subculture revolves around porn.

There are no consequences for any of this. Maybe sometimes they feel sad or "depressed" but there's always a high dollar cappuccino to ward those feelings away for another couple days. I'm sure they have "crisis" vlogs where one of their relationships blows up and they get to explain what happened to their viewers. This probably buys them another couple of weeks of dopamine. Anything to ward those true feelings away. At some point, people lose their humanity. They become permanently warped. Something less than human. But in a sense, and for how messed up everything is, they no longer have to contend with being disturbed at everything's rapid decline. They are permanently inured. This is a fiscally advantageous position to be in. There are millions of wealthy people across America who have simply withdrawn from the fight. They sit around their expensive homes in rural places, waiting for everything to collapse. Those people will eventually get bored. The dopamine hit of fleeing liberal cities to avoid "lockdowns" has not yet worn off. It will be another year or two, still.

Goldman Sachs wants to put people back to work and get them off of telecommuting. The people will be induced to mine more ore for the overlords. A great mass of people working from home has not proved to be the tax revenue producer the elite had hoped for. Sure, deindustrialization is well underway but social trust has not yet collapsed to the point that people can't be lured away from their homes and back to the cities to work some more for Goldman.

The elite probably keep sex servants at their rural compounds. We hear about all the insane degeneracy of the Saudi princes or Australian businessmen. The news trickles through, here and there. The trickle is opening up now though because people who have had operations on their genitals and chests are starting to just brag openly about the nasty stuff they participate in. Why wouldn't this be happening in America? Of course, it's happening here. People don't just move to some $1.5 million house alongside a little creek in Idaho on 3 acres and *not* bring the city's degeneracy with them. Drug distribution has expanded into the rural places. The sex servants go to Wisconsin now. The airlines are being kept solvent for a reason and it has nothing to do with customer wellbeing.

Everybody is getting jabbed in Los Angeles. Cars lining up for miles and miles. Everyone in a rush to die. The collapse was gradual, gradual, and now all of a sudden. The lockdowns are what moved us from a nudge, nudge situation to a snowball turning into an avalanche. Some people just want to have fun while everything goes to hell. Why care so much? That's the reasoning. There are troops deployed on American soil now, to shoot people if need be. But if you're sexy enough, it doesn't matter. You just promote diet pills, squad up with other sexy parasites, and smoke weed until you decide you've had enough of the city and then you buy a $2.2 million ranch outside of Sedona or Casper. The violence these people are doing… They're not just poisoning their bodies with chemicals, altering their bodies with surgery, and living the high life. They take their problems with them. They should be stopped.

But you can't do that. You're not allowed to even want to do that. It's unamerican! And from the other side of the aisle, it's just not even talked about. There's an invasion going on. They want 800,000 people pouring in. It will be 8 million before anything significant changes.

America isn't fun anymore. Everything sucks. You know it. I know it. The spiritual core of this place has been hollowed out by liars and perverts. Doesn't mean you shouldn't try to have some fun. You need it to stay sane. These young, sexy people sell fun. Look! You can get trashed and then go mountain biking. Look! We just ran into Douche at Whole Foods. He has a new girlfriend! What the f! Vacation to Cancun or whatever.

Until we regain the high ground, there will be little rhyme or reason to anything. You'll just have to focus on what's immediately within your control because the broader situation is completely out of control. It's getting so bad so fast that even the lizard overlords are like, "Hey, *maybe* you don't need 3-4 jabs but we'll reserve final judgment for now since there's a good chance we'll walk this back later." The people who have military and technological power over us are immature children and every now and then they betray it. There's like four billionaires in the entire United States who made it over the billion-dollar mark by being honest, good people.

I think it'd be fun to be one of these young, sexy people – for a day or two. I think that might be the point of it. I've only watched a dozen of their videos over the past four years since the vlogging craze blew up. I don't think I'm all caught up in their lifestyles. It'd be fun to live with no consequences for a bit. Have a near perfect body, fill it with cappuccinos, pal around with gorgeous women, and go to the beach. Right? That's what it's about, right? I don't know. I'm getting to the point where I'd rather just go pet my dog, be with my family, and eat homecooked food. I do like to work out. I share that in common with all these sexy Californians. I do love the pump or a bit of the runner's high. I don't like how I feel on caffeine. I don't like shallow conversation. Women with plastic surgery are terrifying, no matter how full the lips or curves. I like the sunshine, I'll admit. It'd be so cool if the sunny places of the world were filled with bookish, self-moderating people. Instead, we have this "children of the sun" nonsense where no one has any impulse control and the whole game is to get in, get money, and get out.

Fellowship Of The Eight

"Look, it's a *fellowship*," said the Wise Wizard. "It is not a bathhouse or bushes by the road stop where deviants congregate. We must not allow him to travel with us."

"I protest. You will need my expertise as an archer. I have a signature move where I whirl around, thrust an arrow into an orc's face, and then use it with my bow a moment later to shoot someone at a distance. I am an indispensable fighter and have keen eyes," said Hairless the Elf.

"Aye, and you've been using said eyes to spy on me buttocks!" growled the Red Dwarf. "From the corner of my eye I caught you at a distance, the day I bathed beneath the waterfall."

"Dwarves don't bathe, Goldseeker. I threw you in," said the Human King.

"Nonetheless, it was wrong of him to do." The Red Dwarf grunted in disapproval.

Tom The Tree, towering over the meeting, groaned out in his ancient voice, "I saw it, too. The elf is as they say he is."

"Please, please we must not infight," said Dodo. "Infighting is exactly what *He* would want."

"How are we sure it's even a 'He'? He could have been born a she," offered Elroy the Elf. "I want to host a reasonable debate about the future of our Fellowship on my neutral platform. Each of you can bring a second. Wise Wizard against Hairless Elf. Who will be Wise Wizard's second?"

"I will," said Hamwise. A single tear rolled from his eye.

Hairless gasped at the betrayal and placed a hand on his own chest to steady himself. "I select Glollum as my second," Hairless declared in his put-on voice.

"What on Middle Earth?!" exclaimed The Red Dwarf as Glollum slunk out of some nearby bushes and appeared at the edge of the Council's stone platform. The dwarves were all in an uproar. The humans joined in the ruckus.

The debate stage was set as the participants rearranged their ornate wooden chairs in the arrangement Elroy suggested.

Elroy clapped his hands loudly and the commotion dissipated by degrees as the participants in the debate took their assigned seating. Many elves from the surrounding village stopped their work and stood as close to the debate stage as was allowed by elven law.

"At our Grand Council today, we have before us the issue of Hairless the Elf and his future status with the Fellowship. Some say he is unwelcome. Some say these reasons are spurious and all that matters is his fighting ability. We call upon Hairless to defend himself today with Wise Wizard as the dissenting party. As seconds, we have Hamwise on behalf of Wise Wizard and Glollum on behalf of Hairless," Elroy announced in a declarative voice. "We look to Wise Wizard for his indictment."

"We *must not* allow Hairless into the Fellowship," began Wise Wizard. "Already we have reports from the younglings that Hairless has touched them inappropriately. Given this behavior and our survey of the facts, it is a near statistical certainty that Hairless will invite certain evils into our midst as the Fellowship progresses in its journey. This must not be allowed." Wise Wizard withdrew a long pipe from beneath his cloak and began smoking the finest barley weed that could be had. He bent far over and offered small Hamwise a pinch of weed for his own pipe.

"What say you to these charges, Hairless?" beckoned Elroy with a strong gesture of his hand.

"I say that you are all being intolerant and we should be as inclusive as possible with the Fellowship. *I* bring certain abilities to the table that you all need."

"To the charges, Hairless – what do you say to the charges? Not the spirit of the matter but to the charge about the younglings."

Hairless scanned his eyes in an ethereal manner across those gathered, making eye contact with all before speaking. "If we are going to defeat Saulon, be it a he or a she, we will need a broad coalition. By expelling me, you are doing a terrible wrong. I have killed many orcs. We need as many beings of Middle Earth as we can get. I represent a crucial fighting bloc that deserves representation. We need to move our Fellowship out of the Third Age and into the Fourth."

"He refuses to address the charge!" growled The Red Dwarf from the audience. "I saw it with me own eyes. He gazed upon me bare buttocks at the waterfall. Think of the younglings."

"Silence, Beard Froth. This is a debate," said Elroy. "We will hear now from Hamwise on the charges."

"I thought this was going to be a debate," pouted Hairless.

"Enough speaking out of turn," commanded Elroy. "Please, Hamwise."

Hamwise took a deep puff of his barley weed and said, "Well, sir, he *did* grab Pippit by the crotch when tossing him up out of harm's way when we were ambushed by the Great River. He didn't *have* to do that. Nor did he have to pat Mariodock on his rear's behind when we made it to shore. He's a strange one, he is. In all my years of interacting with elf-folk, and that is to say I never have, I never heard of an elf doing such things."

"Indeed, it is unnatural," said Wise Wizard in a deep tone.

"I was born this way!" protested Hairless.

"He was, he was," hissed Glollum from his perch on the oversized chair given to him. Everyone gave this strange creature their attention, thinking he would say more but he grew cautious in the face of all the scrutiny.

"What more do you have to say, Fish Biter?" Elroy asked the pathetic Glollum.

"He is good to us, yes, yes. He treats us well," Glollum said, pointing to Hairless. "He makes us feel valued and important. Poor, poor Hairless. The younglings hates us."

"His mind has been poisoned by the Dark Lord," offered Wise Wizard. "He may be of use yet but he has not joined Hairless in these acts. He is innocent, in a way, and will not share Hairless' fate. He only comes to the defense because his mind is broken. He knows not the way."

"That may be so but he was called as a Second, Grey Spellcaster," said Elroy. "It seems we must put this to a vote. We have lost Holodomir at Argonuth, so the Fellowship is Eight. In the case of a tie, we will allow Tom The Tree to cast the decided vote. Raise your hand, those of the Fellowship who believe Hairless should stay."

Pippit, Mariodock, and Hairless raised their hands. All was silent for a tense moment until Dodo raised his hand as well.

"I knew it," muttered Wise Wizard.

"And now, those who vote to expel Hairless from the Fellowship – raise your hands."

Human King, Wise Wizard, The Red Dwarf, and Hamwise raised their hands immediately.

"So it is that we have a tie," Elroy said in his steady voice. "By our ancient decorum and the lawful authority entrusted to me as Top Elf, we must now turn to Tom The Tree – who represents the natural world – to decide if Hairless is to be in the Fellowship or if he is expelled and must pass to the West never again to be allowed near younglings."

Tom The Tree scratched at his beard for a long time, saying, "Hmm" from time to time.

"Well, what will it be?!" an impatient Pippit poked at Tom's leg, hoping to provoke an answer.

"We trees take a long time to think about things. However, this is an open and shut case since I saw it with my own tree eyes. Hairless is indeed who he is said to be. In the Fellowship he must no longer remain."

"Take him away," Elroy beckoned to two elves who had taken up station behind Hairless in the last minutes.

Hamwise broke into tears once again. The Wise Wizard exhaled the last of his pipe's contents and the smoke formed the shape of a soaring eagle. The Human King shook his head in disgust as Hairless looked to him for sympathy as he was being led away. The Red Dwarf burst into laughter and was slapping his dwarf friends on the shoulders in celebration. He chuckled from deep in his belly and said aloud, "Finally, he's gone. He could never stop comparing himself to me!"

You Should Be A Follower of This One Genius

Hey bro, I really care about you. You should check out this one genius. He's very profound. He writes a shit ton of books. He's many things. He's a Millennial whose brain is fried from the copious amounts of media he consumed during his formative years instead of practicing self-knowledge. He's a wry, sardonic almost-Zoomer who only cares about himself, shirks off all authority, and has not been seen in public for years. He's so funny. He's also a near-Boomer who thinks really long thoughts that don't actually amount to anything other than distracting people from their real subversive thoughts and tendencies. He's acclaimed all over the world for his power to help people with surface level stuff like losing weight or getting a job or realizing that things actually matter. He's also kind of gay and tweets at women regularly. He's way into doctrine instead of honesty, which is a nice distraction and cope for me. He's so based. I really care about you and so I'm going to try to shove this guy down your throat without a shred of curiosity when you push back and tell me he's boring. Come on, man. He read Joseph Rogan…kind of. He read Carl Jung. He's got a degree or maybe he doesn't because hey, being self-taught is also cool. He analyzes Marvel movies, which is super pertinent to this Cancel Culture we live in. This one guy, he talks about Jesus and he's bringing a lot of people to Jesus so he's super interesting and you should check him out. You could really learn from him, like how to go to church or that women need a man to act like a man. He's a freaking genius. He is a genius.

You? You're not that impressive. There's something off with you. You don't just ramble for hours upon hours, like I'm used to. You don't have a brain fried by countless hours of media watching. You aren't the representative of some branch of a church and talk about it all the time as a replacement for having a personality. You aren't a smarmy piece of crud who posts to Twitter two-hundred times a day without a care in the world about anybody else. You don't distract people with stories about someone's weight loss or how you realized that things are like this one passage from Nietzsche. You maybe at some point talked about spanking women, which is just weird and I don't understand it and since nobody else talks about it, I just think it's kind of funny and that's it. You don't have credentials and you don't have salt and pepper hair and I just don't trust that. You don't talk about Bible stories and relate them to living in the modern age in a dense and voluminous way. You're neglecting what I really need in order to feel comfortable and secure again. That is just not very profound, sorry. I need tedium in my life so I don't have to think my own thoughts. There's only a level of living that I am comfortable with. I am a hero! I voted Tromp. I am giving money to all the right geniuses. One of them was even *deplatformed.* Have you heard of it? I don't know and I don't give a spit because you don't talk about it and so therefore, I assume it has never happened to you. I don't even guess at the intensity of it or the scrutiny you were put under while it happened because you're just a dude in a room and you're full of yourself. You have made no sacrifices and they would bear no significance upon you, even if you did. Uh, oh. That thought was too insightful and cringe. I need to put you down now, in my own head. You have no long-term plan that I can discern because I don't know, I don't wanna think about that. The way you talk about yourself is really off-putting.

Thanks, no thanks for your time, you douchebag that I secretly envy and want to throw off the scent. Listen to these guys who didn't do anything substantive during their formative years because if I can convince you to slum it with them and that they're the best of the best, then you won't do what it is that you're going to do one day. You should get lost in their tedium and their immaturity and I hate you for seeing how they're immature. I hate you for not making a spectacle of yourself in a way I can gain comfort from. I hate you for not recognizing that I'm superior to you. I hate you for not spilling all your secrets and giving me mastery over you. You need to bow down to me because I know better than you. I am more *something*, I dunno, than you. Why? Because I uh, I am connected to social media. That gives me a lot of certainty. You're boring. You're on some hippy crap. I dunno. You don't do things for me. That's boring. I wish you would just do things for me. I want to love you but you don't want to love me. I need someone. I am so alone.

He Helps

The vista of the Kremlin spreads out before us. We zoom in from the grey skies into a grand window overlooking Moscow Square, or whatever it's called. A man stands at the window. His name is Joseph Stalin. Tens of thousands of starving Russians die every day because of his orders. Here he stands, gazing over Moscow Square, at the height of his powers. He stands erect, proud in the knowledge of what he has done for his homeland.

The grand double doors into his headquarters are opened by his finest soldiers, men who each killed scores of Germans in the war. Stalin averts his eyes from his dominion and turns to greet the small coalition that has come to make their pitch to him.

"Chairman Stalin, on behalf of the Democratic Coalition of Finance, allow me to thank you for your most hospitable generosity during our stay here at the Kremlin," says John Smith, a reedy man dressed in the finest clothing money could buy. His bony hands remain clasped at his waist as he bows in veneration to Stalin.

"Yes, Chairman Stalin, I represent the Economic Foundation for Human Progress," says the second man, an older gentleman named Jacob Smith who bears a pure white mustache and a spectacle over his right eye. "You have been helped us with many travel arrangements that would have otherwise proved prohibitive." This Smith also bows to Stalin.

The third and final man in this small group says to Stalin, "*Russian greeting*, Herr Stalin. I am here on behalf of the Anti-Racism League of Survivorship Interests. While I regret that our chief executive could not be here today, I hope that I will impress you as much as he has. He is currently sick with an illness."

"That is most regrettable," says Stalin. "Please, send him my Soviet best wishes."

The third man, Abner Smith, replies, "I will convey your wishes the moment our meeting is over, Great Leader."

"Gentlemen, seat yourselves. I have fifteen minutes to hear you out. Then I must lunch at the Kremlin Olympic Swimming Pool where our finest swimmers are preparing for their glorious victory at the expense of the pigdog Americans."

The Smiths sit down in three plain folding chairs while Stalin moves from his window view to the considerable throne placed at his writing desk. "Go ahead," he says to the first Smith who spoke.

"Great Sir, we would like to enact certain measures across the Soviet Union on behalf of Democratic Finance. Sir, the people must be able to have credit cards, a recent invention from elsewhere that should be introduced to the people. This will ensure true equity for the Workers of the Union. They must be able to spend money this way. Eventually, we will phase in a cashless society and then they will be real partisans in the global worker's revolution. This is a good idea we came up with in some secret meetings over in Belgium. You have the power to give this gift of consumer spending to your people. That is all, Chairman. Please say yes."

"Nein," says Stalin. "You would turn my people into slaves to someone besides me. I love my people. They are my Russian people and this is our homeland. I cannot acquiesce to your request. As long as I am alive and international monetary interests do not poison me in my bed, my people will remain sovereign under my command. I have expelled from this nation certain intellectual elements that have now completely enslaved the other empires of the world. These elements will remain outside our castle walls so long as I am alive. Now I will hear the gentleman from the Economic Foundation for Human Progress."

The older Jacob Smith withdraws a cigarette case from his vest pocket and offers one to Stalin. Stalin looks to one of the soldiers stationed by, who says, "I have tested every single one. They are safe." Stalin decides against smoking one, anyway. Jacob Smith lights up a cigarette and then says, "Chairman Stalin, your great wisdom saved this land from the German menace. There is a new menace forming and only Economic Progress will save the Russian people. The people must be free to choose who they fall in love with or they will be sad and repressed. We must change the economic incentives around the family and lessen restrictions around divorce, as has been done in the other Empires, so that men and women will stand as true equals in the Worker's Revolution. I beg of you, Chairman Stalin, set your people free with these humanitarian reforms."

"Have I not set them free from the degeneracy of the West?" Stalin asks.

Jacob Smith stiffens suddenly, knowing his life is now in danger. He has been too brash.

"In the United States, these reforms are well underway. People are free to spend however they want and look what they spend on," Stalin says in his steely voice. "People are free to marry however, whenever and look at the decadence of their social order. No, these reforms are of no interest to me. I must continue to keep an iron grip on my homeland. I will not cede power to international interests. I will not hear the last man of your delegation because I already know what this is about. I have made up my mind."

"But Herr Stalin," protests Abner Smith. "Please, mein Fuhrer Stalin."

Stalin signals to the soldiers standing nearby and they take the men away. "Consider yourselves lucky you aren't going to the Gulags," Stalin calls after them.

As they're dragged away, Jacob Smith says to John Smith in a whisper, "Fret not for we have arranged his demise."

Logical Elimination and Murder Robots

Those Boston Dynamics robots you see videos of about once a year are going to be used to hunt down and murder political dissidents. What are the alternatives? Mining applications? We're supposed to be transitioning away from mining. Police work? The money's not worth dumping into the no-go zones that are forming. Nobody's going to burn through a $100k murder robot nabbing some low IQ street thug for killing some other low IQ person. Medical procedures? You don't need robot dogs and walking automatons for that, just a surgical arm sticking out of a table.

No, these robots are going to be hurling themselves through walls, taking small arms fire, and then executing dissidents who don't want their guns taken from them. That or kidnapping them off to reeducation lairs where truth drugs and torture will be used on them.

When you actually go through a process of logical elimination, you realize there is not a single job these things are supposedly going to be used for that a human can't do – except to be meat shields for domestic raids. At the very least, they will replace menial human labor. Maybe they'll be used to set up infrastructure for a colony on Mars but who cares? We don't need a colony on Mars. We need lizard overlords to stop nabbing children in the night here on Earth. We need to know what's beneath the ice down in Antarctica. Ain't nobody give a spit about Mars. We don't need to explore outer space. We need to explore the tunnels under Washington D.C.

To defeat these murder robots, we are going to need access to fossil fuels. You will have to freeze these things or use fuels that generate enough kelvins or whatever to melt their armor. You will need armor penetrating rounds. You will need stuff that the global governments are racing to restrict and then ban outright. You're not going to be able to outrun these robots once the battery technology is efficient enough. The lizard overlords may be too hasty and set these things loose on us while we can still get away on ATVs and dirt bikes but I don't think so. I think they'll wait until the technology is perfected.

We are so far behind on defensive applications in consumer technology. You have few to no defenses against corporate and Deep State power. Bunker homes are still in their infancy. Flying vehicle technology is a thing that has been lazily abandoned to government research even though we're going to need it to defeat the robot and drone armies. It's kind of autistic but drone scrambling technology isn't broadly disseminated. There's a massive array of technological weaponry slowly being aimed in the direction of the American middle class. The open invasion of Central America, Africa, India, and the Middle East into America won't be sufficient. Americans are just too persuasive. Americans will turn sufficient numbers of these foreigners against the elites. Far less than the civnats promise, though. A mop-up job will be undertaken. That's when the murder robots come into play. For as extreme as police training and "continuing education" programs have become, they still can't convince the police and US military to openly murder citizens. They are "purging the ranks" and remaking everything into a Communist/globalist attack force but this takes time, is slowed by whistleblowers, and faces internal resistance at every step of the way. Beyond this, they have to wait until a good chunk of expelled veterans and police are past fighting age – which also takes time. Murder robots can make up the time. Public relations-wise, the military can even be set against the murder robots, to some extent, and a lot of dissident deaths can be swept under the rug in the fog of war.

The world controllers are having these conversations all the time.

There is literally no reason a robot should exist.

Learned Scholar and Respected Professional

Dr. Rajmandi stood at the lectern in front of ten thousand of the world's top scientists, ethicists, engineers, immunologists, surgeons, psychiatrists, and law enforcement agents. The applause his entry had been greeted with died down and a hush took over the assembly.

"My fellow real human beings," he began to say, in his thick Indian accent. "Sorry, one moment. I am nervous." He bent down to tie his shoe, which was greeted with laughter. "There, okay," he laughed. "My daughter says my shoes are always coming untied. Forgive my eccentricities. They come with being a genius. As I was going to say, my fellow real human beings, the past years have tested us all. We have battled this thing back and come together as a human species. It gives me great pleasure to share with you the results of my findings. First of all, speaking as a scientist, this whole disease is cow dung."

The crowd roared to life and everyone stood to their feet and applauded Dr. Rajmandi.

"We all know it is cow dung," he said. "It is made up. It does not spread the way anyone in the government says it does because it *does not spread*! The media lies about everything because everyone in the media is morally compromised and blackmailed by the child and human trafficking rings. And that is *cold, hard science*. I have a medical degree from Johns Hopkins University and also a graduate degree from Harvard Medical. I also have a degree from Yale. And I have two other degrees: one from Oxford and one from Princeton. I have the highest scores on every single standardized test I have taken, including my space science examination at NASA. You can believe me when I say, this is not a real disease. It is the bad kind of cow dung, as we say in India, where I had the highest college entry exam scores in the entire country. Also, as the man who owns the most carbon credits on the planet, I will say this: the government simply stole death numbers from different categories and assigned them to this contrived disease. And you can trust me when I say that. I am a scientist!"

The crowd of the most intelligent people ever clapped with renewed enthusiasm and several roses were thrown on stage for the virtuous performance.

"Speaking as a scientist and as an economist who got a degree in economics from MIT, the computational evidence clearly shows that we should be reopening everything and never closing anything through government force ever again. Sorry, but that is just what the science says. Trust me, I am an Indian scientist. But more than that, I am a global citizen with all of the best grades anyone ever earned from any institution. Furthermore, we need to stop blaming white people for everything. This is not my opinion. This is what IBM's quantum computer determined after a lengthy meta-analysis that has been fully peer reviewed by the Department of Justice's highest standards. It is simply science: stop blaming white people for everything. We need to come together as global citizens and help white people. Again, this is not my opinion. We have the hard data and scientific proofs to support this conclusion."

The conference attendees slowed in their clapping but only because they were beginning to tire.

"I am also a doctor and I have fought on the frontlines of medicine for thirty years and I have to say, we need to stop killing babies. The science simply does not support it. You cannot morally kill a baby. A scientific analysis done by a crack team of diverse scientists and computational forensic doctors, assembled in Iceland by the United Nations and European Union, released a 6,000 page report that says you are a stupid, evil idiot if you support abortion and you should be locked up for life if you have one. This is not moral philosophy or religion. This is actual science. I am the foremost authority on this subject on the planet and no, not just because factually I have the most prestigious degrees and published articles on the topic but because science itself has given us irrefutable certainty of my authority. Please, you may stop applauding me. I implore you to take your seats. I only have one more thing to say before we end this conference."

The 10,000 experts gradually resumed their seats. Dr. Rajmandi drank from his glass of water and peered out onto the assembly through his thick glasses. He set the glass back on the wooden stool near the lectern and with tremendous gravity, spoke once more, "One last thing. Speaking as the foremost scientist on the matter, we must get women out of the workforce completely and entirely."

The women in the audience immediately stood to their feet and clapped. Many women tore off their lab coats, police uniforms, hospital scrubs, and so forth. Many dozens of women began leaving the venue, proclaiming loudly their liberation. The psychiatrist women threw down their bottles of pills. The police women cried and let down their tight ponytails, decrying the shameful way they had attempted to live as men.

"I can see you women have been liberated," an enthused Dr. Rajmandi cried aloud into the microphone. "Go forth now. Science has set you free. This isn't just my personal opinion. We did extensive studies using the most advanced technological equipment and funding from all the world's governments to arrive at this theory. Women sour into miserable wretches the more years they're employed. And this is the bad kind of cow dung! Science does not support women in the workplace, at all, whatsoever, ever again. Come out of your bondage and slavery. You no longer have to live in the intellectual Dark Ages. You are no longer oppressed. Go now and spread the word. Science has set you free. Ladies and gentlemen, on behalf of the Council On Foreign Relationships, Global Economical Forum, The Opening Society, Central Intelligence Agenda, United Nationalities, Fabian Social Club, the Rothschild Buttbung Corporation, Raytheon, Lockheed Martinship, Goldman Sacks, Bongo of U3, the Sus-sexes, the

Clinton Foundational, the Podesta Child Research Facility, Black Lives Mingle, Jeff Bozos, and SERN, I want to thank you for liberating the world using proven scientific methods. We have now entered a new Golden Age. Speaking as a scientist but also a brown man, remember, the disease is not real, we need to stop being mean to white people for literally no valid reason that has ever been proven by science, and women now don't have to work anymore ever again. Goodnight and may the light of Science shine upon you!"

Canadian Crimes

Sandy blonde haired Canadian e-girl with bright red lipstick and giant whore hoop earrings leans into her Joe Rogan style microphone and says, "Rich Daddy, thanks so much for joining me today. Wow." She gives him a knowing look, like there's some kind of inside joke they are aware of. This is her father, and their repartees go back a long time. This impresses the audience and provokes envy in them.

"Hi, well, yes – it's certainly rather interesting to be here," says Rich Daddy in response. He is an unwell man rapidly approaching his 60's. He is dressed in a tailor suit selected for him by his wife for the special occasion of appearing on his daughter's podcast.

"So, Daddy, how are you doing?"

"Not good," says Rich Daddy bleakly.

"What would you say? 10%?"

"Yes, that's about right. I'm at about 10% or 15%." Tears well up in his eyes. The audience is immediately sorrowful. Their great hero has been through so much.

"Yeah, and that's a lot better than before, huh?"

"Yes, I'd say so," the man responds, on the verge of tears.

"But we agreed we're not going to talk about that, huh? We've been over it and people know."

"Yes," the man mutters through his trembling fingers tracing his quivering mouth.

"Okay, so Rich Daddy, we have a listener question. The listener asks, 'Rich Daddy, I'm an insecure Canadian coomer who's in his 20's. What should I do?'"

Rich Daddy shifts in his seat, like a role has come over him. "Well, that's awfully vague but that's *okay* because sometimes you might have to be vague to get what it is that you want expressed in a way that others will draw from and learn in a substantive way that provokes real change. Okay, 20's and a young man. Well, you've got to have a *plan*. You need to know what you are going to do in five years. You need to know what there's meaning beyond chaos and it's not that easy. There's danger. You could be in trouble. You don't know."

A man in his 30's steps into the recording studio and interrupts the recording.

"Who the fuck are you?" hisses the e-girl with nauseously bright red lipstick.

"I'm a grown-ass man. Shut your little whore mouth for a second," the man growls.

Rich Daddy tries to stand up and defeat this new dragon in his midst but the stress of the moment causes him to break out crying and he covers his face with his trembling hands. He lets out a pained moan. The audience is so sympathetic to his heroic, meaningful suffering. He is like Atlas carrying the weight of the world.

"You stupid bitch," begins the man. "You're pumping Rich Daddy for insights like an advice column. He's clearly not up to this. And you," the man points to the sobbing older man, "you should shut the fuck up for a good while. You've had miserable moral failure after miserable moral failure for years now and yet you persist in making it about yourself. Your mind has been ruined by psychiatry and by neither provable nor disprovable psychoanalytic logic loops programmed into you by elite institutions and intellectual superiors you called 'mentors'. Now you're unleashing this madness into the world and because 99% of people can't track it and pin it down for what it is…"

The man trails off for a moment's hesitation as the e-girl starts pawing at his pants zipper. "You're a *real* man. I want to suck you into me," she moans. She shimmies her $200 push-up bra as far up as her A-cup breasts will allow it to and her black sheer blouse shows the edge of her greying areola.

The man pushes her away, giving her severe psychological trauma. She hangs back at the edge of the area left visible to the two-camera setup in her studio. She starts making self-conscious faces at the cameras, hoping to draw ridicule upon the man from her audience.

"Cut that out, bitch," growls the man. "Back to you, old man. You've made a career off of helping people do basic shit, like realize that meaning is actually a thing and publicly reading letters from fat liberals who lost a bit of weight or saying men are men and women are women. Yet, you've denied people the most fundamental insights that you are capable of. You have denied people a real moral compass to be able to navigate the all-out assault on freedom that is currently being carried out. Despite you, we are only just now beginning to win."

"Well, that's just not true," Rich Daddy protests weakly before collapsing back into sobbing. The audience out on the Internet starts to feel pure rage and already have thousands of rebuttals prepared for this cruel and sadistic interloper. They scan about furiously on the Internet to find the man's contact details in order to send him manipulative, fifteen paragraph long emails they hope will leave him creatively drained and suicidal.

The man points at Rich Daddy and says, "Look at you, weakling. Your mind ruined by pharmacology and psychology. You are another could-have-been white champion reduced to utter dirt and then paraded around the entire world to demoralize anyone else who would dare scale the mountaintop. You keep people locked in a prison. You make it as sumptuous and covert as possible. But anyone worth a damn knows what you have done. We know when you said, 'I can't.' You have not begged for forgiveness for a single one of your trespasses. That's cause you're a sellout now. And your whore daughter mines you for Dear Abby nonsense to advance her own interests. She's a Lilith. A demon. You've spawned weaklings. You whimper and whine. Your wife whimpers and whines. But because there's a bit of Nietzsche or Bible stories in it, suddenly it's not whimpering and whining. You failed. You broke your mind. You expended your lifespan's main shot imprisoning people in liberalism. You're a suicide case. And no amount of appeals to 'getting tough' or 'the Hero's journey' will change that now. And since you are a liar and a manipulator, your whore daughter's podcast is forever cancelled. She will be put in isolation, using your funds, where she will detox for the rest of her children's childhoods."

Rich Daddy cries and cries. His face turns beat red and he looks like he has the flu/coronavirus. He attempts another protest, "This is authoritarian. Copernicus warned his contemporaries about this."

"Shut up!" says the towering figure. "You have misled enough people. You have turned away more people from the right cause than you can salvage for the rest of your life. You have relinquished your free speech because you single-handedly bought years of time for the Managed Decline and the globalist takeover. Everyone is just going to have to rely on an actual businessman, Tony Robbins, for their weight loss and money advice. We've destroyed all the globalist publishing outlets that were hyping you to the high heavens. You will no longer get any of people's UBI or their stimulus checks, as we've done away with all that while you laid around and pretended not to pity yourself. You have to just hang out in the woods with your daughter and your boring, ugly wife. Go ahead and tell yourself you're exactly like Solzhenitsyn, fading off into obscurity or whatever else will allow you to sleep at night."

Rich Daddy is escorted out of the house, with his entire family, and is led to his vacation home which is stocked to the brim with survival goods and healthy livestock. There Rich Daddy lives another 12 years before dying of heart failure or his testicles dropping off or something like that. These are the happiest years of his life. And once or twice in that span, spared the worst of their psychological tendencies by being barred from accessing the Internet, he and his family members reach a *real* catharsis that puts them within spitting distance of realizing the harm he's done to their family and to the world – before collapsing back in to their shared delusions (which he planted in them in the first place).

The audience is angry, as they perceive he was wronged, but they're literally all too chickenspit to challenge the power structures that put him out to pasture. Yet, they feel superior.

Women In The Military

Yeah, I got a bit of a bad boy streak. I make fun of women a little bit. Women in the military? That's gay. Yeah, I just said it. If a woman in the military is defeated in physical combat, she automatically belongs to that man. He owns her body. Why not? She signed a cheap, slutty contract to be in the military anyway. The military owns her body. Why shouldn't the male who defeated her in combat? She's his property now.

Women need to learn a little bit of something here. No, you're not strong and independent. You're just a snotty, mean witch. And if you're childless over the age of 30, you're practically useless to the world. You're a spinster, not a fighting force. And I'm happy to enter the Octagon with *any* woman who disagrees. Don't hide behind your computer and type snotty stuff at me and try to get me run out of civilized society. Just back up your words with your fists, tough lady. Anytime, anyplace.

Yeah, kind of a bad boy. I put people in their place. I try not to, though. I try to be a kind sweetheart but there's only so much of that you can do before you start to turn in on yourself. It gets to be too much. You lose sleep. You play it too nice. You don't get places. You turn down opportunities. We should start a fighting promotion for female veterans: fight a man in the Octagon and if you somehow win, he has to pay off your debts for nothing in return. If you lose against the man, he owns you and can put babies in you whenever he wants and you can't divorce him unless he's trafficking your kids or I don't know, breaking beer bottles over your thick skull. It's not like the Chinese would be any nicer to you, out on the battlefield. There's a lot of rape coming to Canada. They stir fry dogs alive. You won't make it, girl. Join my fighting promotion instead. We offer women a way out of their debt, just like the military does. Only, we don't turn everyone into self-loathing alcoholics like the military does. Something to mull over.

Women tend to be depressed. The thrill has gone out of their lives. Maybe they want to be raped off in some Middle Eastern hellhole, that's what a man at the bar speculated to me one night down in Colorado. I'm not sure about that. But women do want some thrills. They want to be dominated. The social landscape is so bereft of dominating men, given Consent Theory and other mind viruses, that women resort to being meat puppets for the American ghey empire in order to be swept off their feet. Women are out of control and live with no consequences. They can't fight worth a spit. Sure, they can be trained to kill, shooting guns or flying drones, but they're out of their depth. If they're going to be out of their depth, we should at least funnel them back into marriages where they'll be reined in and quieted. We have the will to dominate. We can apply cultural pressure. The spectacle they're making of themselves can be ended.

True News

Been reading a lot of books lately. Been thinking about stuff. How America is falling apart. Keeping what's within in my control in a good place. Improving the sleep, bit by bit. Watching the critters grow on the small farm here. Listening to some elevator music.

Writing is work. You sit and you shape something, off in private or out in the living room on the couch where there's a house full of life. You have to focus in. You have to shut out the noise. The world is so full of noise. You have to be careful who you internalize. If you internalize leftists, you begin to hate yourself. You begin to put yourself under false premises. You deny yourself true happiness and you aren't even aware of it. You get those little bursts of comfort that come from surrendering your spirit, your life force. The voices of the leftists are subtle. They put doubt onto your grand designs. You internalize this as "depression". You feel less motivation to accomplish anything. You give up on living your own life and look to the computer or the TV to give you an animating purpose. To get rid of these voices, you have to reduce your contact with their sources.

The Republicans have this huge problem with constantly being concerned with what the Left is doing. They're always responding by pointing out the Left's hypocrisy. Would you believe what the Leftist superstar did this time?! Rather than promote from within and get behind their most competent figures, the Republicans prefer to greedily self-promote and promote the Left. It's tiresome. You can't listen to these right-wing figures too much. A bit is necessary because the Left holds the high ground. But too much and then you're self-defeating yet it doesn't feel that way because you're mimicking what those on the right with the largest platforms are doing. This is insidious. I don't hear anyone talking about it. The activist bent of the Left is the real beating heart of what they're doing. The cat scratch battles on Twitter and Facebook are just the window dressings. Imagine if the right did internal trainings instead of just going, "Can you believe the *zinger* Tucker Carlson scored this week?" Meanwhile, the Left puts everyone in cages.

Let's talk some more about how you eschew those leftist voices that nestle in the unconscious. You have to dredge them up in your quiet moments by *paying attention* to your own thoughts. You close your eyes, shut off distractions, and then listen to the narratives and dispositions of the thoughts in your head. How are these thoughts influencing you? You have to be curious about them. You can't just weigh in with an ideology. That just increases conflict. You want to listen attentively and then offer good arguments and general feedback that will move those thoughts into more truth value. The Left feeds off of fear. Fear drives these thoughts. You can't be too harsh with yourself for feeling fear. You have to dance with the fear a bit. Keep a healthy tension. The thoughts will move out of fear if you maintain your focus long enough. Then things resolve and you're more or less sorted, for a time. We get leftist fears pumped into us from all angles: social media, government employees, family, friends, neighborhood, traffic signs, advertising, chemtrails, xenoestrogens, electromagnetic poisoning, and especially the DMV and airports. You have to maintain the sanctity of your sanity and not allow leftist excuses to bridge into your innocence and corrupt you from within.

Today I helped a newborn lamb get over his cold leg by wrapping him with a towel and then putting him under a heat lamp. This is more amazing and notable than anything any leftist politician did. This is real life. It is wonderful. It is difficult to maintain this ground because of outside influences but if enough people commit themselves to maintain and *augmenting* this ground, we will wipe evil from the face of the Earth. It's going to take a long time. You also have to keep in mind the money cycle. You shouldn't be overinvested in doofy assets the government can manipulate and distort at-will. The government can always stop welfare payments or food handouts. That's probably the bottom of the barrel. You want to be invested in crypto, friendships, family, God, and your creative capacity in this life. The government could put literally everyone in prison, as it seems to want to do all the time, and people would get creative about escaping. It is the essential commitment to living as a free, proactive person that breaks the prison bars over time and sets the world free. You don't want to give up on that in yourself. The weight can drop off your body. The psych meds can go down the drain. The dead-end job can develop into the something. The environment can be scrubbed of plastics and harmful chemicals. The borders can be closed. All good things can come to pass but you have to slog it out and never give up on yourself or the truth.

The Moral Improvement of Women

Women are in a sorry state. You know this is my point of view! I am here to help. Women have learned a bunch of nasty strategies for advancing global totalitarianism, indulging their impulses, and undermining all the greatest achievements of men. They were taught these strategies; we'll just say by Satan.

I'm going to name a few mean female archetypes or strategies that we can begin to deal with in order to make everything better for everyone.

The Frame Dominator – Somewhere along the way, this woman picked up that she needs to run things. She tries to run everything. She interrupts men. She talks first. She thinks her opinion is valued first and foremost, *especially* when there are more intelligent people in the room. This is her defiance. It is also a terrible burden on her. She's just pushed the consequences down under. Privately, she is exhausted from keeping up this posture. It's not natural. The way you deal with her is to catch her when she goes to speak first. At first, she will hate you for this. That is because she doesn't trust that you will demonstrate the competence she has had to demonstrate, up until this point. Remember, she has unreasonable expectations foisted on her for years and years. She will test you to see if you will actually carry the weight. Men are built for carrying weight. Stay limber in your mind and you will carry the weight dynamically, no problem. Ease up, even for a moment, and she will crush you as she's been trained to do. Don't show a moment's weakness. Why would you? You're not weak, anyway. That's just leftist self-doubt. Your great grandfathers won wars and such. The Frame Dominator will give you her worst hell right away. Imagine Candace Owens grabbing you by the testicles and saying, "You're not man enough, boy". How do you get this crazy, aggressive woman to back down? You shoot electricity through your testicles. You generate it in your heart and then you shoot it down through your balls. Her hand will get shocked by your sheer power and she'll withdraw her hand. The worst ones will re-grab your balls once or *maybe* twice after that but they all stop. A woman Prime Minister is simply a woman who has out-feminism'ed all the men in her country. Trump came in and showed em' all.

The Word Twister – This woman contests the meaning of words. She antagonizes this way in the hopes that you will lose track of the initial disagreement and spin out with her into her world of manipulative emotions. Too many guys take the bait on this. Come on, guys. She's pulling you out of words with meaning and into the witchcraft of her feelings. If she wants to rake you over the coals on the meaning of words, simply know the definition of words. It doesn't cost you much to keep a non-globo homo physical dictionary copy from pre-21st century in your house and look through it once in a while. Don't use online dictionaries. They change definitions to pave the way for globalism, all the time. And remember, she doesn't actually care about the meaning of words.

She wants to nitpick you because you're starting to get the upper hand, because you have better arguments, and she can't stand the thought of submitting to your authority. That's what this is about. So, don't get too autistic on dictionaries, either. But a bit helps. Our autism shields us from being impulsive women slaves. Trust your autism. Try to have *pure autism* sometimes. I may write about pure autism somewhere later in this book. Also, never let *The Word Twister* switch words in that will paint you in an unflattering or insulting light. No, you're not a creep. No, you're not a pushover. No, you're not mildly gay. No, you're not a dunce. She's choosing to try and squabble with you, after all. That means there's something she's stupidly trying to extract from you. That means she secretly thinks you're smarter than her. And high chances are that you *are* smarter than her. Don't bully her with that fact. Just don't lose your head when she starts picking at words like a nervous hen.

The Seductress – You don't need sex. You need fertility. Fertility is conceptual. Sex is physical. Fertility requires a whole set of responsibilities and best practices, as a breeder. Sex just requires jungle voodoo. When you gain power in this life, women will quite literally slide into your lap. They want your resources. A fool and his resources are easily parted. You have to have a farmer's mindset with seductress types. They're threatening you with ruination. Some can be tamed, others can't. The ones that can't be tamed are given over to the Devil and are not worth your time, anyway. They often have STDs and will make you pay double the price: soul sucking and physical agony.

You have to be practiced against seduction. What's your self-talk when the Internet or TV puts babes in front of you who are showing parts of their breasts or rumps? Do you simp out like a whimpering suckling? Do you feel greed and neediness? Even a flash of it? Or do you feel anger? Do you feel the bonds of fraternal love wrapped around your body like chainmail? The seductress is attacking you. You need chainmail, my brother. Don't let her pierce you like that. She's evil and nasty. It's not worth it. It never will be. You'll just be parted from your resources. *Maybe* you'll get a pregnancy out of her but she'll either take your children from you one day or your kids will be incomplete losers because their mother forged them out of something other than true love. It's harsh but it's the price The Seductress will make you pay. I'm not making you pay, by pointing it out. I'm on the outside at a distance cause I want nothing to do with these types. Keep the farmer's mindset. Look for a breeder. Keep your brotherly chainmail on. When you find a sweetheart, you will take the chainmail off of your own accord and by your brother's watchful eye. And choose a *winner*. Your friends may be a bit loserly, since packs of young men these days tend to bond over the wrong things, and they may be intimidated by a winner girl when she first comes on the scene. All women take a bit of taming because the state of Boomer and Gen X father to daughtering was absolutely abysmal. Don't let your friends' feelings of intimidation overwhelm you. Test your mettle and if she's about fertility and can be tamed, take over. Be a man, damnit. But never ever does a breeder come your way by fornicating or flirting with your friends. That's a seductress.

That's all I want to say about this subject, for now. I want to jump around to other stuff. You can't write too much of this stuff in one place or you will get typecast. I'm an all-arounder! I'm a humanist, or something. Peace and love are my mantras. I'm into sports and comic book movies and paying for things with my smartphone. I'm a stupid dipstick! (I almost just cursed.) I just swipe my phone on the card reader pad and then look around as everyone admires my stylish face mask that I bought off Newegg. I feel nervous and insecure around conservatives. My corporation keeps it breezy with a business-casual dress code and that's alright by me. In the summer I am adventurous and go to the city park. I try to pet people's dogs. Narf!

Zombie Apocalypse

There is a full-blown zombie apocalypse ensuing. The Orange Man was just barely holding the center together and now everything is descending into anarcho-tyranny. We live in a will-to-power world. Hordes are flooding in, aided by the military and major corporations. Small businesses have vanished. Deaths of despair are sky high. The intelligence agencies are pursuing their vendettas with impunity. The stock market is going to tank. Real estate is going to tank. People are going to be waiting in line for food. They will trade being injected with gene therapy for a loaf of bread. There will be raiders attacking farm operations. Underground bunkers are being built. Elon Musk is pulling an *Interstellar* and trying to get a bunch of people off this rock. Full blown genocide is being perpetrated against the one group most capable of stopping all this.

You have to be ready. You have to stay fit. You have to be entrepreneurial. You'll want to stay on your toes but relax now and then because you need your rest. You need other men, now more than ever. You need the bonds of friendship and trust to carry you through. You need to try for a family, so you'll hit gears of effort you didn't think were possible. Give your life force to the next generation. Expend the cell energy. You'll want to get out of the cities. Those will be death traps. They already are. Look at the skyrocketing crime rates. The cookie is going to crumble. Judgment Day is coming. Something big is in the works. We have all been primed for it through media and now the world controllers are going for it. Band together.

The zombies will come. They're probably already near you. The military has been running exercises for years where they cut off the food supply to a town by drone bombing all the fields and poisoning all the water in the area, then they swoop in armored Humvees, and they trade food for the locals giving up their genetic material via biometric scanning devices. The elite are harvesting your body for information they'll use for life extension, disease resistance, cognitive improvements, etc. The military exercises involve firing on "zombies" as the zombies attack the vehicles. The zombies are desperately hungry people. That's it. You are in a medical caste system now. You didn't know about this? Or you aren't able to do anything about it? That means you're not making it to the breakaway society. The military has been trained to deal with you. They've had 20+ years of genociding people in the Middle East. Their trainers, several decades longer than that. The zombie hordes are coming to where you are and they are going to turn you into zombies with them. The average 80 IQ person has nothing to live for. No higher ideals. Not anymore, given the state of corruption and irreligiousness he lives in. He lives to consume. He is overabundant in the environment. The wildlife was fed by the generations before you. This doesn't take some genius level conspiracy to pull off. All you need to know is a little bit about wildlife biology, wildlife population control, and then dash in a bit of hatred of humans and you've got a devious mind capable of making this mass psychotic fantasy into a reality. Everyone has had a part to play. The masses were given their scripts, the lines to read, the ways to behave by the zombie apocalypse movies.

You or your children, probably both, will be fired upon by military troops because you rush a supply convoy on its way back to the underground bases. They have vehicle mounted weaponry to microwave you like a potato, blow out your ear drums, shred all the tree cover you intend to fire from, and drones with mini missiles to blow up your children wherever they're hiding as you carry out your act of desperation. The military guarding these elite also have space cannons in low orbit to wipe out militia strongholds in Idaho, Wyoming, West Virginia, Wisconsin, and so forth. They also have pathogens waiting in the wings that they will unleash as uprisings threaten their power grip. People who have undergone gene therapy treatments will be "primed" for these pathogens and will be among the first to go.

All of this will come to fruition if you don't adopt some low-level tolerance for conflict. You have to be willing to take off the blue mask. You have to be willing to protest. You have to be willing to put verbal pressure on quisling Republicans. You have to be willing to go talk to people who are at least somewhat reasonable and try to hash it out with them. You have to draw a line in the sand. You can't allow yourself to be induced into the track-and-trace programs they're calling "passports". You must not allow yourself to be disarmed. Stuff like this. A bit of terseness now will save a lot of horrific decisions and scenarios in the future. There is not going to be some magical Soviet collapse of yesteryear where the baddies simply give up, money cycles to more competent hands, and there's more freedom in the world. This has been fully accounted for. The Soviet Union collapse was a controlled experiment and the relevant findings were extracted. This is going to be a prolonged, bitter decline immune to convenient Austrian theories of economics that leave us feeling bubbly and warm about humanity.

The true horrors of totalitarianism have never been exhibited in America. There was no mechanized land invasion here. Our landscapes were not turned into moonscapes by shelling. There are few to no mass graves anywhere. No city or town here has really ever had to be rebuilt other than maybe a few barns being fired by British troops long ago. All of the atrocities have been pushed far away to Siberia or the barren plains of China. Or the jungles of SE Asia. Or the sands of Greater Israel, wink-wink. Anyone who has fought back against the global elite ended up getting smoked *far away* from the cameras.

The bloodletting is coming home to roost. And they're going to use murder robots to do a lot of it. Did I mention that? A nationwide electro-magnetic tracking grid with drones and Boston Dynamics robots deployed to quell tax livestock found in non-compliance? Yeah, I think I talked about that already, at least on a livestream sometime. How can people not see this confluence of factors? How can people be so inured to mortal danger? People just don't seem to understand what death is about. Maybe they have not thought on it for very long. Certainly, people do not know the sweetness of life. They do not fully or even partially comprehend the horror of the spoiling process. The real murderers that need to be profiled on those endless TV shows on demand are not the random killers and rapists who roam rest stops and such. It's the scientists in medical facilities, the military brass in heavily fortified bases, the bankers in their estates with their rituals, and the people who are already spending more and more time underground, drinking blood and torturing children for magik. There is the real taste of evil. They think what they do is done with the utmost secrecy but it reverberates out and angels hear at a distance. The evidence of their crimes is everywhere. They send out men in dresses and makeup and we laugh to steel ourselves against the "nightmare fuel". Who has the sensitivity to *truly know* the agony the tortured children endure? People don't want to read into things like this. They say it is traumatizing. There is truth to gazing into the void too long and the void gazing into you. I wouldn't want that for anyone. I am talking about the nature of evil and the knowledge of suffering. When you know the goodness and sweetness of life, you can see the dark underside. And both of these will push you to do what is right. The zombie apocalypse is here. Steel yourself and do what it is right. You have permission, if you needed it. I give you permission. Let your conscience give you permission. Do what is right. Live free.

King Kang vs. Japzilla

King Kang wakes up to The Tokens' *The Lion Sleeps Tonight*. The Boomers in the audience feel the CIA programming kicking in. They feel sympathetic to him as an archon of democracy. He's basically a proud, intelligent black man like Obama or Will Smith or Sydney Pottier or Samuel L. Jackson or Michael Jordan. That's good. King Kang gets up from his resting spot against a cliff and he walks around scratching his butt. He dips his head into a giant waterfall and sniffs around like an innocent lamb. He's kind of adorable.

A little half-brown girl who looks kind-of-Asian walks out into the jungle carrying a King Kang totem. She is the daughter of the most genius ape researcher in the world, who reminds Boomers of Jane Goodall. The little girl holds up the totem to King Kang right after he rips a tree from the ground. What is he going to do? She's so tiny. He could crush her without even trying. He rears up from the totem the girl is holding, which indicates to us that they have a special bond, and he hucks the tree he's holding like it were a toothpick. It flies almost a mile, because that's nothing to King Kang, and it hits the sky! Some display panels crack and tumble and it is revealed to us that King Kang is in a digital enclosure on an island. He's been kept distracted in this place so he won't go rampage around like a monkey.

On the other side of the planet there's a funny black guy who's like a suburban Bernie Mac. His name is Mac. He's at a fancy base in Pensacola, Florida where The Corporation is building some top-secret stuff. Mac is a little bit overweight and nerdy. He has Airpod earbuds in his ears and Nike shoes on. He is wearing inoffensive working-class clothing. He is sneaking around the big fancy base. He's podcasting while he's doing it. He's making references to Nazis and Hollow Earth Theory. This is pretty funny and quirky. Then Japzilla attacks!

Japzilla swims in the ocean with his huge blue energy-charged scales sticking up. Jet fighters with proud black queens in them try to take him down with missiles but Japzilla rips the jets out of the sky. He starts shooting his blue beam of energy out of his mouth and destroying The Corporation's base.

Everyone is panicking and running away from the base. Mac slips into a top-secret underground area when he thinks nobody is watching him. He's running like a fat person down the hallway and stumbles upon two super soldiers who we resent because of their upper body physiques.

"What the frick are you doing here, boy?" growls the white super soldier.

The larger, black super soldier stops his companion dead in his tracks by putting his hand to the man's chest and saying, "Hold it. He cool but we should still kick his ass for being down here."

They start to move toward Mac when Japzilla's blue beam of energy blows a hole into the base and kills the super soldiers. Their blood and guts are scattered everywhere. Mac is shaken but he emerges from some wreckage coughing and wiping dust off from his working-class clothes. He checks to make sure his flask of grape drank strapped to his chest is still okay. The walls of the top-secret area he was trying to get into are torn away. Revealed to us is a huge red orb that looks like some kind of reactor.

"What the frick *is that*?" Mac yelps. "Damn, I better get out of here. I'm hungry, y'all."

The CIA's news network, CNN, plays some quick news feature to us about how Japzilla killed eight people in his latest attack. It is indicated that he killed some illegal aliens and black people. That means that King Kang has to be scuttled into combat with Japzilla to bring Japzilla under control.

The little half-brown girl convinces King Kang to get on an American aircraft carrier. King Kang is sedated but only at 88%, a favorite number of the Illuminati. The Jane Goodall lady is giving orders to Navy admirals because she knows more about King Kang than they do. They go along with her plans because she's empowered and important. Her words really matter, especially to

Man Candy – her boyfriend/super soldier employee. They are in the aircraft carrier's command center.

Japzilla attacks again! He's swimming like a torpedo or a shark in the ocean, straight for King Kang. Some proud black queens in jet fighters fly around and shoot missiles at his blue energy-charged scales on his back and this time Japzilla expresses a little bit of annoyance. He rips them out of the sky and they eject safely so they don't die and become a statistic. King Kang is revving to fight, like LeBron James before Game 3 of the 2016 Finals. He's *pissed*.

Man Candy tells Jane Goodall that they need King Kang kept in his shackles to complete the mission. That means that King Kang can't fight! She's mad at Man Candy for pretending he knows better than her and she's proven right when Japzilla upends the aircraft carrier and King Kang starts to drown in the ocean. Everyone is underwater when Jane Goodall saves little half-brown girl and *also* pulls the lever that releases King Kang from his shackles. Now King Kang is really pissed. He swims up and bumps the aircraft carrier, making it resurface right side up. He hops on it like a surfboard. Japzilla swims up and gets on the other end of the aircraft carrier. They start punching each other. Japzilla punches King Kang. Then King Kang punches Japzilla. Then Japzilla punches King Kang. Then they fall in the water. Japzilla pulls King Kang down in the water to drown him. King Kang has an innocent look on his face as he's running out of air. He didn't do anything! There's some sad music but then Jane Goodall realizes that the Navy admirals, one of them is LGBTQ, can use *depth charges* to resurface King Kang. The admirals dutifully call out the order to use those charges. They explode in an impressive ring of CGI and suddenly King Kang resurfaces. He was able to be jostled free from Japzilla's grip, even though Japzilla can easily outswim depth charges.

Jane Goodall tells all the admirals to make the fleet shut off its engines so that Japzilla feels as if he won the fight. This is good emotional awareness. The admirals do what she says and then Japzilla comes up to the surface of the ocean to be sure that he won. He pokes around a little bit and then leaves, sated. King Kang is passed out because he doesn't swim so well, a feature of his species. He just needs to rest a bit. He tired, y'all.

Turns out that there's some Jurassic world in the center of the planet. Mac figures this out when he goes with a white teenage girl into The Corporation's super base. The white teenage girl is the daughter of an important, liberal, handsome guy who works for The Corporation.

The new mission is to go down into the Jurassic world to tap into the energy there using space shuttles. It's called Hollow Earth down there, a nod to Internet conspiracy theorists (thanks, CIA!) So, Jane Goodall directs the fleet to go to Antarctica, where she jokes that Hitler lives and tic-tac spaceships fly out of. King Kang is put into an arena area and eventually he wakes up. He decides he wants to go into the center of the Earth and be back home in Hollow Earth/Jurassic world. So, he swings like a monkey down through a tunnel and everyone in their space shuttles follow him, including some bitchy woman with an amazing body. She's brown but her dad is an evil white man who leads The Corporation.

They go through a gravity portal and everyone is on LSD suddenly. *Come On Baby, Light My Fire* by The Doors plays for a minute while everyone trips out and the screen flashes. If you slow the movie down, you see single frames telling you to murder white people and burn farms to the ground. Then King Kang is happily back in his home of Hollow Earth.

Meanwhile, in the only other subplot of the film, Mac and Jailbait (the white teenage girl) have penetrated deep into The Corporation. They're trying to learn the conspiracy secrets. Like, maybe there's aliens and Nazis or maybe Trump really did get his second term. Something like this. They go up a tunnel in the infrastructure of the base and their bodies get a little too close for a second, which is awkward but funny. They conk heads, which is also funny. Then they come into full view of Hirohito, the Japanese 2nd in Command of The Corporation, and El Hombre Blanco (who's the dad of the sexy-bodied brown woman). Mac and Jailbait get apprehended for their free thinking and get sat down in chairs right next to the command console of the Mecha-Japzilla that The Corporation has built. Mac looks up through the window, as he grins and bears the boring dialogue of Hirohito and El Hombre Blanco, and notices the red energy reactor thing that he saw before in Pensacola, Florida. He mutters to Jailbait, "I seen that thing before. Remember, in my podcast?" She nods quietly because it is dangerous.

In Hollow Earth/Jurassic world, King Kang has to protect the squadron of shuttles following him from some snake dragons that attack them. He does a good job. He brutally breaks their bodies apart and sucks the brains out of one snake dragon. The little half-brown girl waves to him from the forward windows of the space shuttle he's in. King Kang is really happy with that. He runs along his homeland, which is at the heart of our world meaning he predates us and we're all descended from him. Sonny & Cher's *I Got You Babe* plays loudly. King Kang is happy. He's in his element. He keeps going where he is instinctually driven to: a massive temple that obviously other Kangs built. Inside, there is a huge, crude tomahawk axe that has magic blue energy power, like Japzilla does. He puts the axe into a slot on the ground and this charges the axe.

Somehow, up above in the world of men, Japzilla knows that the Kang temple has been activated. He shoots his blue beam of energy out of his mouth directly into the ground. He's clearing a tunnel to Hollow Earth! The sexy-bodied brown daughter of El Hombre Blanco decides she needs a core sample from the temple. The corporation needs this so that Mecha-Japzilla will be able to shoot *blue* energy out of his mouth instead of red energy. Blue energy runs the world, not red energy. Then some big birds attack King Kang and the crew of humans that are with him in the temple. Sexy-bodied woman just barely gets the core sample in time and then tries to fly off, shooting King Kang with a machine gun. The bullets annoy him and he smashes her ship into flames. The big birds fight over her charred body. Little half-brown girl is in danger from a big bird but Man Candy saves her, proving he is a good surrogate father for this child that somehow belongs to Jane Goodall. This allows Jane Goodall to focus more on her career, which is always a good thing.

Japzilla finishes shooting the laser hole into the planet's hollow core and King Kang decides he wants to go *bang* with Japzilla one more time. He goes through the reverse gravity field and flies upwards to the Earth's surface, to the city of Hong Kong. He lands gracefully on the ground and does International Sign Language to Japzilla, saying, "Let's fight, nigga." He has the battle axe this time, so he's feeling more confident. He's like Francis Ngannou fighting Stipe Miocic for the second time: surer of himself and armed with the big guns.

Japzilla whirls around and his tail lashes a skyscraper full of people. Thousands die but nobody notices. He punches King Kang. King Kang punches him back. Then Japzilla hardcore punches King Kang. King Kang tries to use the battle axe but Japzilla punches him so hard in the balls that he falls over and spits out blood. Low blow! King Kang punches Japzilla in the balls pretty hard back and Japzilla keels over, knocking down a skyscraper and killing tens of thousands of Asians in the process. Nobody cares. Jane Goodall, little half-brown girl, and Man Candy watch from a distance in their space shuttle. They're rooting for King Kang!

In the other subplot of the movie, Hirohito has powered up Mecha-Japzilla through a human-to-machine mind interface and is getting the blue energy from the core sample uploaded to his fighting machine. El Hombre Blanco unzips his pants and urinates on Mac, who's tied up to the chair next to the command console. "Yo voy a votar por Donald Trump," sings El Hombre Blanco. Jailbait cries because she finally understands the plight of black people. Mac weathers the urine with a grim look on his face.

Back in the action, Japzilla has basically punched King Kang too many times and now has the ape pinned to the ground with his claw foot. King Kang is defeated! He signs, "I can't breathe" many times over the course of eight minutes and 46 seconds. Eventually, Japzilla opens his mouth at King Kang but just roars, basically saying, "Cut it out, dude." King Kang roars like a proud black man in defiance and now a pecking order has been established: Japzilla is alpha but King Kang is kind of alpha, too.

Japzilla starts walking away to go back into the ocean. Mecha-Japzilla comes flying in out of nowhere and kicks Japzilla between his buttcheeks. Mecha-Japzilla hits way frickin' hard and is making easy prey out of Japzilla. Hirohito goes to use the blue energy but the blue energy overwhelms his interface, frying him to death, and then the Microsoft A.I. takes over on Mecha-Japzilla. The giant robot starts shooting lots of blue energy everywhere, hitting Japzilla some.

King Kang is basically super exhausted and he definitely got suffocated to death. Jane Goodall tells Man Candy that they have to fly down there and save him. They land the space shuttle on his chest and then climb down. Man Candy holds little half-brown girl in a loving manner as they run away from the space shuttle that's set to explode. It explodes in an impressive way that suggests actual white or Asian people did the CGI programming and King Kang *roars* back into the fight just as Japzilla is about to have his jaws ripped apart the wrong way.

All Star by Smash Mouth starts playing and everyone feels cozy. Mac breaks his binds and throws El Hombre Blanco down a flight of steps. He yells, "Welcome to Earth!" as El Hombre Blanco's body shatters on the concrete floor a hundred feet below. He then runs to the command console for Mecha-Japzilla. Jailbait yells at him to *do something*. He pulls his flask of grape drank from his working-class shirt pocket and dumps it all over the command console. This short-circuits Mecha-Japzilla just as it was going to shoot a laser from its tail at King Kang.

"You did it!" yells Jailbait as she places her hands on Mac's shoulders and gives him a little congratulatory shoulder rub.

"Black Lives Matter!" roars Mac, throwing a power fist into the air.

Mecha-Japzilla doesn't function all the way perfectly anymore and this is just the opportunity King Kang needs to chop off the robot's arms and legs with his battle axe. Japzilla is panting and heaving, leaning against a Hong Kong hospital skyscraper with several maternity wards being crushed under his weight. Screaming Hong Kongese babies are falling out of the windows but in the Chinese version this is edited out.

King Kang finishes off Mecha-Japzilla by ripping off the robot's head and eating its brains: his signature move. Remember how he did that in Jurassic Hollow Earth to one of the snake dragons?

King Kang walks over to Japzilla and helps him up. Jane Goodall and little half-brown girl wave to them as they start walking away together into the sunset. They need to go chill in their home world, which pre-dates our own, until they feel good enough to fight Mothra or something else. Steppenwolf's *Born To Be Wild* starts playing and King Kang sheds a single tear because he finally has a best friend.

Globalization of Dating

By 2030, 45% of women aged 25-44 will be single[1]. Male virginity rates are rapidly rising. A bunch of bad stuff is happening. Men are supposed to be totally sterile by 2045. It's hard to fathom total sterility across the globe. Surely, the Mongolians and the Indians will still be breeding. We're glutting up the natural environment with glyphosate, phthalates, and all manner of other xenoestrogens that are completely destroying our hormonal profiles. Testosterone drops 1% a year, across the West. If you have worn skin lotion or sunblock in the past year, just imagine the chemicals from it going through your bloodstream and directly to your testes – attacking them with psionic lasers. That is what it boils down to.

The women. We have got to do something about the women. They won't breed! Or they select for bad boys or hold out years of their fertility for the perfect pretty boy to come along and save them. This cannot continue. When you dig in to what the workplace is truly like for a woman (and women are in the habit of lying and so you have to divine it by reading between the lines) a woman is constantly overwhelmed by a full-time job. Women are just not up to it. They cave under the pressure. Every single one of

---

[1] https://www.cnn.com/2019/08/29/economy/single-women-economy/index.html

them, ever. The absolute best women you can name are women that don't actually work full-time. They do media gigs, occasionally. Or they write books, which you can take breaks from whenever you like. Also, you can't name that many great women because exceptional women in the market are exceedingly rare. I am talking about moral quality here. What woman wades into the marketplace and holds on to her moral center? She is an *extreme* rarity, not the average.

Let's talk about the globalization of dating, since that's what this bit is supposed to be about. The other day I was watching a heavyweight champion in MMA nearly getting his head knocked off by a powerful dude from Africa who, athletically speaking, is one in a billion. Quite literally. He would be top 1% of sporting achievement in whatever sport he'd have been trained in since childhood or even teenagerhood. This African fellow would have a sporting chance coming in against this American champion simply by doing one single training camp of six weeks and then wading in with haymakers. That is just how it goes when you can punch like a titan and you're as strong as an actual water buffalo.

This white American champion from Ohio is a likeable type. He's ex-champion now. He's a little older than me. He's Croatian, originally. He grew up riding bikes around the neighborhood. He played baseball at a high level until he threw his shoulder out or something, like half of those guys do. He's a salt of the earth type. Relatable. A little bit of white guilt going on but nothing too extreme, just enough to make his way into a globalized sport.

This fight between Ngannou, the terrifying but soft-spoken African, and Miocic, the firefighter from Ohio, was hyped and hyped because the promoter, Dana White, and his money men know just what a breadwinner Ngannou would be if he could unseat Miocic. This is symbolic. A white, blue collar man from Ohio getting his head lopped off by the absolute prime force out of Africa – a man who attempted to illegally invade Europe seven times before finding some kind of legal status. The backstory was that he was cruelly and unfairly dumped in the Sahara six times to starve to death before he made it through. He worked in a *salt mine* as a child. This is the stuff of wet dreams for any globalist out there. Since you can't make the arguments for globalism work, just go with the emotional-symbolic angle and justify Ngannou's existence in the West on account of his otherworldly physical talent. It's merit, after all! Why shouldn't the most physically gifted human be entitled to a shot at the *world championship*. He's a cash cow. It's a feelgood story. You're a racist prick if you question his legitimacy as champion because all that matters are his physical gifts.

Don't get me wrong. I'm sympathetic to Francis Ngannou as UFC heavyweight champion. Same goes for Israel Adesanya as middleweight champion. And Kamaru Usman as welterweight champion. They are phenomenal fighters, best in their divisions, and the pride of Africa. That being said, they would not attain champion status were it not for the infrastructure, nutrition, legal environment, and general freedom that they have been offered by the United States, specifically, but also by New Zealand (Adesanya) and France (Ngannou). The fact remains that mixed martial arts is an American and Brazilian invention. It is *somewhat* an international sport but primarily American in nature. We could also throw the Japanese in there because they reliably ride along for everything exciting that Europeans do. They have good taste!

This is a similar path to dating, albeit imperfect since MMA has always been more international. "Dating" is primarily a post-WWII, American invention. Courtship is another matter, spanning the globe since time immemorial. But *dating*, that's American. There was a *bit* of international crosstalk in the early years of dating (1946 to 2000's) but that was mostly with Europeans. You had certain things come out of this American cultural phenomenon, like romantic comedies, trans-Atlantic leisure travel, and the resort industry in the Caribbean, that were folkish expressions of European self-involvement. Dating was a thing unto itself. Then came along the compounding effects of bad immigration policy across the West at the same time that online dating took off. On top of that, now there are "dating apps".

Nobody alive who has followed MMA for the past 20 years, as I have, can honestly look you in the eye and say that the hype surrounding the vast majority of the MMA champions is as *intense* as the hype of those champions in the early years: Chuck Liddell, Randy Couture, Fedor Emelianenko, Tito Ortiz, Vitor Belfort, and a few others. Sure, there are tens of millions, if not hundreds of millions, more fans than there were twenty years ago. By sheer volume, the noise around today's champions is louder, but the intensity is not. This is the same kind of thing as the NBA. The best players of the 1980's and 1990's were all-time icons who paved the way for the media capture that the NBA attained in the 2000's and 2010's, as it internationalized. Magic Johnson or Patrick Ewing meant more to their respective cities and were well-regarded to an extent that the modern elite basketball players simply can't replicate. This is not the fault of modern players, by and large, since we're talking about systemic changes and cultural consequences downstream from gigantic government programs...but maybe this is a bit their fault and perhaps we'll go into that. Back to the fight game, those early champions *belonged to us*. Tito was a Cali guy. Couture was the wrestling guy who did all the wrestlers proud. Fedor was the Russian, or something. Vitor and Royce Gracie were the Brazilians. These guys belonged to their tribes and the lines were delineated. The last nationalist champion figure was probably Conor McGregor, as all the Irish went out for him in the early going, and he became an internationalist as his star faded. He benefitted from all the groundwork laid for him by the early champions, peaked right as the UFC was gaining full media capture, and fizzled out as MMA switched to Syndicate Mode. Now the whole thing is a well-oiled machine, as makes logical sense for *fighting*. After all, it's individual guys from *wherever*, beating each other's brains in. This is not some competition of meaning. But it is objective in the sense that there's finality of outcome.

As mixed martial arts, at the highest level, has become more and more internationalized, the champions are not products of their unique cultural and societal backgrounds – like the Olympics of a century ago. If they have the physical talents, the fight IQ, and the durability, there is a *machine* for them to go through in order to gain entry into The Syndicate. The Syndicate is international. There's *Fight Island*. There are feeder leagues on TNT and other networks. The mixed martial arts game is a system unto itself, untethered from national concerns and beholden only to restrictions on international travel. The fight game, as the basketball game, is more beholden to international airlines than it is to a nation of people. The Syndicate stages wherever fighting is a rich man's fancy. The only tribal aspect to it now is black ethnochauvinism in the service of globalism. There are no American champions anymore because the unique Americanness of boxing, wrestling, and the pugilist ethos has been pilfered from the American system and incorporated into a corporate system that extends to every corner of the globe. Whether Francis Ngannou can reliably vote for less government simply doesn't matter because he makes moneyed interests richer. Same goes for all the other champions of *all* of the sports, at this point. You're extra pleased when the man is a clear nationalist or Christian, like Tom Brady or Tyson Fury, but a champion is no longer an outcropping of a coherent, regional culture. A champion is an interchangeable fixture as part of a larger, promotional enterprise. The word "champion" loses some of its meaning.

You are watching a mop-up operation of all ethnic fighting, herd tendencies in white man. He's the best at making civilization but he's not the best verbally, so he is pulled down by Judeo critical race theory. He's the best at war, but he's sort of dead even or at a mild disadvantage with the incredible physical prowess of the black race, so the matchmaking is always slightly tilted against him. He is the best craftsman, so he must be drowned out by trade with Asia and its limitless pool of cheap labor. There are all these vulnerabilities to exploit.

The same goes for the total siege that white women are under, currently. We are a far cry away from, "I wish they all could be California girls". The beauty queens of yesteryear were representative of the distinct regions of America. We knew Jersey girls from Annie Oakleys. We could generally infer where blondes were from and where brunettes were from. We had Spanish roses and Georgia peaches. With every woman was nuance, cultural complexity, and distinction (but not higher intelligence, remember). Oftentimes a California girl would win beauty queen. Every now and then, a wispy brunette would take it. African Americans similarly had their own distinctions. You had your brown sugar. You had your "mamas". There were other types I'd name but it'd piss off too many people. It's true, though! And my *real* brothers out there love me just for mentioning it.

The excellence of white women in their dating suitability and the heights they rose to in their sexual market value was capitalized, media saturation was achieved right as mass migration effects hit, and now we live in a steep decline. It happened not only to white women in America but also Hispanic and black women, but we're focused on white women for now. Suddenly these women find themselves competing with every other woman in the world, because of dating apps, and they find themselves approached by every other type of man in the world. The logic of dating used to involve folk pathways to finding each other. The homecoming queen was a point of distinction that would attract certain kinds of young men. The physical environment played a huge role in whether people could reach other or not *and* it put limits in, important limits. You were compelled to someone who had a similar accent as you. Women naturally found their way to men who worked in the same fields as their fathers. The conceptual environment that guided dating was filled with all sorts of mechanisms to ensure compatibility and block out outside, aggressive interlopers. I'll write about this again toward the end of the book.

The Stipe Miocic vs. Francis Ngannou fight is a perfect example of all the subtlety of an intimate dance being lost. Everyone knew Ngannou was going to blast Stipe's head off. In centuries past, Ngannou would have slaughtered hundreds of men on his warpath to becoming a regional king with a large domain. The fight was compelling in that it's a slam-dunk highlight of a man getting his head blown off. Matching two Croatians against each other is no perfect guarantee that there will be a chess match of a fight, which is the more compelling and artful dance for less impulsive viewers, but it is a higher guarantee. Ngannou is the perfect McDonalds of mixed martial arts. He will knock everyone's head off.

Dating has become that way. There has been a huge race to find the McDonalds of dating. First it was the online dating sites, with pictures to peruse, then the dating apps which *emphasized* pictures, and now there's easy access to Instagram, OnlyFans, Facebook, and Twitter prostitution. Danielle Bregoli turned 18 years old, immediately opened an Only Fans, and made $1 million dollars in 6 hours for a couple bikini pictures of herself. She is the "knock a man's head off every time" of dating: the ultimate prostitute. She's not pretty and so it's not a perfect analogy. Also, there's a lot more honor in training as a fighter and willing oneself to victory over a difficult opponent. Dating is in an open freefall and the same can't be said about mixed martial arts.

The erosion of the nationalist, folkish aspect is sort of the emphasis in all this. The logic of the digitized, globalist systems has centralized human interest and attention onto extremely specific dilemmas. The white bread white man who wears a cross is pitted against the most savage, overwhelming warrior kings from the outworlds, again and again until he is hacked down by the sheer volume of the outworlds. The "California girl" is pawed at by all of the villagers of the outworlds and compared forensically to only the finest of physical stock the entire planet can supply until she either caves in and submits to an outgroup male or she withdraws into schizophrenic self-absorption (feminism).

It's an aside, but icons of global convenience are constantly psyoped by the system itself to ward off anyone who could break them out of their mental prison. A global icon who turns against the system retains, for a bit, the *heat* of having been endorsed and promoted by the system's marketing and public relations firms. He or she is therefore highly effective, for a narrow window of time while the system withdraws its resources and fires up its smear agents in the media, at bringing worshippers out of their trance. This happened with Donald Trump, most famously, and with others such as Michael Jackson, Roseanne Barr, Kanye West, Sean Connery, George S. Patton, Smedley D. Butler, Tom Selleck, Mel Gibson, Tupac, and others. Fame is an array of deceiving notions, sentiments, dispositions, inner voices, suggestions, and anxieties that shroud a person over time and turn them personally against truth. Donald Trump is probably the person to have emerged most robustly intact from this deluge.

I would not strip any of these foreign-born or foreign citizen title holders of their rank and privilege, not directly. The UFC corporation has *had* to internationalize, due to the erosion of freedom in the United States. If state by state authorities have their own heads so far up their own asses with self-hating liberalism that they can't shake out of the fog and throw out some incentivizes to bring the circus to their state, then that's their deal, isn't it? Or if they're too cowardly to stand up to the federal government psychopaths, that's their deal, isn't it? The federal government isn't going to send troops to engage against state troopers or whatever because a governor flips the White House the middle finger by disregarding a bunch of BS executive orders that only hold up in cat-lady courts. Las Vegas continues to be able to draw big money, one-off events because the Mob runs Vegas and can cut away any red tape and bribe any commission for short durations. The federal government actually works this way but on behalf of Big Tech and international bankers. Barring a Freedom For All approach, which demonstrably worked in the past but may not be tenable anymore given demographics, it'd be a nifty approach doing what the Mob does with Vegas or the Swamp does with DC by *legally* getting voted into office and then doing the loophole trick on behalf of working families and small to mid-sized farm operations. It would work out the kinks of the fight game, to some extent, and certainly provide relief to men and women in America getting *crunched* by globalism in the dating markets. Ban pornography. Assign special counsel to Hollywood and Silicon Valley. End welfare. Close the borders. Stuff like that.

Another thing is that under globalism, resources flow to the most inefficient – sorta. Globalism is its own inefficiency, so those who are the most efficient at making use out of inefficiencies are the ones that get all the resources. Think of Bill Gates. He was not the best innovator of his time. His operating system didn't make the most sense. There were plenty of one-off boutique machines that beat out his. What he was best at was using the state to promote his operating system. He famously captured most of the nation's school system contracts by the mid-90's. This was the defining move to make in an era of completely unchecked government expansion in education spending. And it turns out that Bill Gates has become more and more evil over time, continuing with his mad variety of contraptions built on top of false foundations. He has a machine that takes pure sewage and turns it into clean drinking water, instead of telling the natives to not defecate in their water and fencing off water supplies they prove incapable of tending to. He has a nuclear reactor with different coils that a woman kinda sorta designed, while demanding the entire planet reduce its energy consumption as he increases his own – year after year. Next, he is going to actually blot out the sun with the help of some government, after shilling solar panels for years.

The globalist sports leagues funnel money, because of the taxpayer money they get (which is different from the real incentives I alluded to earlier) and because they serve as money laundering, human trafficking, prostitution, and drug running fronts for international crime syndicates, to largely empty-headed consumerist minorities who waste the money on greedy wealth management firms, oddball real estate deals, and on franchising vegetable oil driven fast food chains that make everyone die early deaths. Oh, they also spent a great deal of their money on prostitutes who advertise on Instagram. Globalist dating funnels attention to Satanic witch women who are willing to undergo cosmetic surgery and display their bodies to millions of strangers in exchange for attention and endorsement deals, on the "innocent" end.

The big myth is that Big Business is somehow reflective of competence. Ayn Rand pushed this. She did not make the basic distinction that fundamentally moral business owners have a hard time scaling because they're unwilling to use the state, which is bringing a gun to a knife fight against your fellow business owners. Or maybe she did but she certainly didn't highlight it all because I read all of her books except *Anthem*. Once the first few businesses in the area lower standards, everyone else has to follow suit or get wiped out. Minarchism and anarcho-capitalism fundamentally only work in ethical, high IQ population groups where everyone staunchly honors the gentleman's agreement not to run to the state for unfair competitive advantage. Since nobody cares about that agreement and now our country is full of people who wouldn't otherwise exist in the gene pool were it not for government programs, we have to figure out a way to peel back Big Business and Big Government that involves more than just trying to convince idiots to put down the gun in what *should* be a knife fight. The best solution right now seems to lie with business owners or would-be business owners devoting themselves to populist statecraft in order to rein things under control. Trump was effective and he could have been *far* more effective had he done the right hiring, a problem he was set to remedy in his second term (I have it on good sources!) The damage he would have done to globalism would have been irreversible. Maybe it already is irreversible, as some say. Point being, other "mini-Trumps" are having a go at it, now. Some of them are stupid phonies who just want to helm Big Business deals themselves. But some of them, like Paul Gosar, are bonafide and genuine. You need people of real moral spine who won't take the proverbial "trip to Israel". Eventually, it'd be nice to have people who don't even have to take the "trip to D.C." We're a long way off from that. A few generations, I'd reckon. And we'll see how far this Goldman Sachs cabal is able to set back true human progress, now that they have their hands on the levers of power. Maybe Bitcoin blows them out of the water and takes the work off the backs of Christian patriots. I think not, but I've learned one thing: don't bet against decentralization. It always finds a way.

The actual most efficient people have an (by design) impossible time justifying themselves as the real value creators of the world to a globalist culture and economic system. The good thing is that you, as an investor, can look for this severely undervalued person, dating prospect, and perhaps some kind of alternative sporting league, if we're staying within the scope of this thought train. Invest in the future you want your children to have, not the massively lucrative short-term projects Bill Gates is spazzing out over. Why invest emotionally in Francis Ngannou, metaphorically speaking, if you know he'd probably be deported back to Cameroon in a just society? I'm not saying I'm going to try and impose that on him. The world needs to change. He'll enjoy his millions for a long time to come. But we can't turn a blind eye to the knowledge that he's partially dumping that money into some go-nowhere, feel-good MMA school in his homeland and has hired some amoral, at best, wealth management firm to cut him a check once or twice a month. And hey, it could be worse. We've come some distance from 1980's sports stars blowing it all on cocaine, used car dealerships, and Mexican-made flood zone mansions.

I think about this idea of the actual-not-most-efficient having all the resources funneled to them in a sick society. Consider a real estate agent. She's 39. She's a single mother of one boy who she gave some nonsense name like Wilderness. The father is not in the picture. Her brother is in the military, is on a vaccine distribution force in a foreign country, and has adopted two Third World daughters. The real estate agent was a bartender until her early 30's until welfare allowed her to get a business degree from a liberal arts college. She made $150k last year, her first year in real estate. She's set to make $500k this year. This is an actual person, by the way. I didn't make this person up. Can we honestly say this person has a true command of $150k to $500k a year? You used to have to employ a bunch of people and be a fixture in the community to make that kind of money. Now you just raise your open hands, or boobs, into the air and catch some of the money that grifter millionaires are hemorrhaging as the American empire staggers into full collapse. And *you know* she's just turning around and spending that money on Amazon and Starbucks. That's the other thing with female spending patterns: they're as dog crap awful as their voting patterns. There *is* such a thing as socialist spending. Businesses are not just doe-eyed innocent lambs hanging out in the marketplace, waiting for some kind soul to trade with them. Sex sells. Addictions sell. Consumerism sells. Women buy all this dumb stuff and the world gets measurably worse. I think of this woman's inner dialogue, "Thanks for the money, you idiots! Manicures, BMW crossover vehicle, Amazon Prime everything, Starbucks, and soccer cleats for Wilderness!" She does almost next to nothing, in the vast majority of real estate transactions, and gets 3% of the sale -which she hands *at least* 1.25% of over to Jeff Bezos and whatever freakazoid is running Starbucks these days. Most female spending is like this. Public school teachers are probably the worst of the worst. Them or overweight female judges in deep Democrat territory. Can we honestly say some dumb chub who needs diabetes meds and cusses out white male prisoners during their hearings because Netflix programmed her to is sincerely adding $200k a year of *justice* to the world? No, not at all. Doesn't this kind of undermine her legitimacy and break down the very meaning of a judgeship itself? Yes, yes kind of. What do we do with this information? Nothing illegal, obviously. People are figuring out smart contract stuff on the blockchain. I think it will be *ok*. But don't take my word for it. Try to reckon with these facts and influence society in your own way. I'm doing what I can.

For whatever it's worth, I like Francis Ngannou a lot. He's a charming, sweet person who has a successful future. When he punched Stipe's face into smithereens, I was somewhat happy for him and the fight outcome aligned with my expectations. As a person, he's a charmer. I just think he would also punch *my* face in if he knew I didn't appreciate him showing up to Europe and sucking up the resources the way he has. So would most of those fighters. So would most of the top "e-whores" or whatever you want to call them. Well, they'd try but I would forearm block them deftly and then call the police, as everyone should the exact moment anything remotely stressful happens.

The Cowpoke Companion

Aren't we having a good time? These books I write are unlike others books, by and large. Here at the Franssen Farm, I am reading about four books at the same time. They're good books, don't get me wrong. I'm learning about esoteric history, hormones, the environment, diseases, and political theory. A couple of the books even feel like a *conversation*, which is kind of what we have in these books I write. I don't have a specific aim in this format of book other than there is a strong conversation component. Some people would say these are collections of essays or a blog in book form. I don't agree because there are themes that bind the different sections together. A blog from me would look different. Maybe "essays" but then I throw in a lot of entertainment. We have fun here.

Personally, I need a break from the BS. The world is filled with terrible news. Civilization is obviously in steep decline, though there are definitely whitepills here and there. There's some cataclysm that is being enacted and there will be murder robots. Fertility is dropping 1% a year. Real estate developers and health inspectors keep ruining everyone's lives. Soon the military will be ruining people's lives. Can't we just go back to an occasional lawyer, here and there, ruining lives? 100 million people just *showed up* to America in the last 30 years. Some subsection of that horde will train to become lawyers. It's nasty out there! We need respite, at least I do. But not the fade-into-oblivion kind that the corporations offer. I'm talking about dunking on women. I'm talking about jive talk. I'm talking about squirrely stuff. We gotta have some fun. That's why I roll with my guys: they know how to have fun. Having fun and laughing in the face of certain peril is masculine, right? It's the gallows humor that I talked about in… *Make Self-Knowledge Again.* Yeah, our lizard overlords are springing death trap after death trap but all that is gay and lame. We want laughs. We want mirth. We want long conversations, late into the night. We want levity. As your cowpoke companion, I'm here to offer some. Maybe I will call this book "Your Companion For The Decline". I get tired of that word, though, because I am ascending. I am getting closer to God. I am living better. I am learning new ways to be better to the people I speak with. I am becoming more efficient at my work. Having a family helps, a lot. You'll want to make it the highest priority, if you haven't yet already. Having a family changes everything. Join the gene pool.

I think of that PBS radio show with Garrison Keillor, *A Prairie Home Companion.* It's a slice of Americana, liberalized of course, that is a decent representation of the Minnesotan sentiment. That show has had a large hand in keeping Minnesota blue. Now the Somalis will keep Minnesota blue. Them and the riggers in Milwaukee. When you listen to Garrison's show, you feel cozy. He's going for that 1920's and 1930's variety show feel, when the nation was entertained by radio and it was the dominant medium. He joins a folk band to sing old songs. He weaves a liberal web that is cozy and homey. There are scripted dialogues and skits. The whole thing is, or at least was, done to a live audience. It is done very tastefully, even though it's brainwashing propaganda and Keillor will probably burn in Hell for all of eternity.

My books in this style are *kinda* like that, sans the evil propaganda part. They're useful in harkening back to some natural sanity. Garrison is always plugging people back into that old-time Democrat *feeling*. You get to go back to the day when liberalism was a kind notion and the body bags hadn't piled up. I'm not harkening anyone back to some kind of conservative "pre-crime" era because what I represent has never ever hurt anyone. Don't let the propagandists hear that. They'll flip out! We know how they'll flip out, so we don't need to go over it once again. Maybe read *Rise And Fight*, if you want to know what they do to hurt us and throw us off the scent. I remember the goodness and promise that America held. It still holds it; we just live under an empire of Lucifer – with Baphomet doing a lot of the heavy lifting. These books here plug people into the good vibe. Into the goodness and tenderness and strength of the old European theater of intrigue. What wonderful people that came before us. The Greeks, the Italians, the Scandinavians, the pre-War British, the Germans, the southern Euros, and so forth. And we extend beyond them to the gypsy and Slavic countries and beyond them, even further. The world was so filled with goodness, not that long ago. It is through television and then the Internet that the evil ones have been able to rip people out of a state of nature. Here, we will keep the flame alive.

Conservative Badass

He steps out of his 2500 level truck. It's massive, with a canopy that makes it look like an SUV. He sort of bark-greets me. His pregnant wife and kids pile out of the rig. I like him halfway, right away. Yet, I note that something is off. He does come and shake my hand, which is a big plus in my books. His wife doesn't go for the handshake, which I like. He does a threat assessment of my place. I wait for him to be done with that. He takes a good long time, relegating me to making idle chit-chat with his wife. I try not to but she's looking at me, expecting it. What the frick. This is weird.

We get to walking and talking a bit but he's distracted. Clearly, he thinks he runs the show. He's like a surgeon in a trauma ward: all business. He does whatever he wishes and expects others to constantly follow in-tow, picking up the slack wherever he lets some out. He's a real executive type. No problem. I've been around these guys before. They're value-adders. It's the subtle aggression toward me that I am picking up on. He's used to men being more submissive and deferential than I am. He doesn't see my value.

We keep walking and talking and I do entice him back into the convo, here and there. It is the man that needs the information, not the woman. Women don't play "telephone" all that well. They're always editorializing. It's their default. It's just nature, don't take it personally. The guy wants me to know he's *real outdoorsy*. Oh yeah, he's felled a big buck in his time. He's a *real hunter*. Alright, I can sort of get with that. Never mind that the country has been totally flooded out by people from poacher societies and that our mega-fauna, if you can call it that, is in complete mortal danger. Last summer I drove north of Boise on a Sunday late morning and it was *thousands* of trucks with fresh Idaho plates driving down from the mountains back into the city, bumper to bumper for about forty miles. This was in *Idaho*. All tough guys. Conservative tough guys, weekending in the Great Outdoors. So strong! So confident!

Then I tell the guy about a nice success I had, since he broaches a topic in my field of expertise. He exclaims, "Atta boy!" to me. Now I'm irked. Calling me "boy" on my own property? I'm tempted to type a curse word here. That's like patting a guy on his crotch or pulling a dog's tail. Big guy, big hunting outdoor executive guy, what is wrong with you?

You see, he's a high money earner. He earns $200k a year, on salary. He's a salary man. He doesn't know how business negotiation works. He hasn't had to learn that stuff. He's a conservative, which is good and praiseworthy, and he has a big family all decked out in Patagonia clothing. He made sure to text me before he came over to tell me they had a big of shopping to do at *Cabela's*, which notoriously overcharges for literally everything down to the ammo.

I've known this stuff for a bit. I start in on how I fought for the right cause. I tried to stop a steal, so to speak. He clams up. What tiny bit of curiosity was in him has lifted. Yet, I keep going. I pull his wife into it a little bit, which is my own small power move. I held her at bay, as any decent man should, until this Conservative Tough Guy decided to call me "boy" on my own property. I knew he was going to clam up the moment I mentioned this stuff. I continue, even though he signals he's not interested. Oh, you hunt big bucks and you got a big truck and you're 6'3" in boots? I'm in flip-flops and I stood with the best men of our age. Thank me for my service, Executive Man. He can't handle it. He crumples a bit. I flash just a bit of a look that signals to him that I know he crumpled. Our deal isn't going to go through, from here. He would want me to believe it was *I* who shot the deal. After all, he's the salaried man. He out-earns 95% of the planet. He's got the best hunting rifles and looks you in the eye when he shakes your hand firmly. But I know it was *he* who shot the deal when he called me "boy". Just couldn't help yourself, could you? We're three years age difference. Five years, at most. You couldn't help yourself. I won't take it, from you or from anyone. I earned my effin' stripes in this life. And I didn't dump my earnings into adornments and *lifestyle*, like you did. I'm gonna let you know, a little bit.

That's the thing with these high dollar conservative Tough Guys. They don't actually put anything on the line. They just retreat and retreat. They always cede ground. Boise is an effin' strip mall now because these guys just can't help themselves. Hey, the stores are semi-conservative. Wow! Great! We get to consoom a little longer at the stories that play country music because Dr. Dipshit brought his four children family up from California to buy a condo cash. Eff you. I put my physical safety on the line to try and get dingleberry Brian Kemp to do the right thing. He signed that voter ID law just now because I went to his mansion, out of my own pocket at hefty expense, back a few months ago. Now you're strutting about *my land*, calling me "boy" and walking around like I should behave like one of your nurses. So, I'm going to let you know. And it's not passive aggressive. I want people to be who they are. You need to be able to breathe and with Steve, you're always going to get to breathe. I'm a Freedom Man. You're free to charge around, doing your brahma bull act with your fit family. I dig the executive vibe. I love the truck. No envy here. I got a good one, too. But it's the calling me "boy" on my own land that I don't abide.

I'll never forget that line of trucks, pouring south from places like Council and McCall down through that narrow highway carved into the rocks leading into Boise. *Tough guys!* Big trucks! Big ammo and big guns! But you tough guys didn't show up to the actual battles, like I did. Keep on bitchin' about the gas prices inching up. Keep on putting plastics in your children's bodies. Keep on ignoring voices like mine, because I don't grow out a big beard and fellate the troops. Keep on packing into Jackson, Bozeman, Coeur D'Alene, Kalispell, Cheyenne, and Bend, you big tough guys. Keep listening to the bro country. You're going to make a bloody mess of things when it all goes down and the World Controllers are *well aware.* I still love you. I'll take you *any day* over the libs and the hordes but don't think you're King Daddy when the deal goes down. I'm King Daddy and you will learn to be my friend.

I bid the guy farewell. He gives me a brief, weaker handshake than when he showed up and turns his back to me instantly. His wife is completely unaware of what has just gone down. She's a breeder. It's okay. This guy knows he and his will always be safe with me but I don't abide his grift. Maybe one day we'll meet again but he's had all he can take. All it took was me mentioning fighting for the actual real things in this life and he melted. Very weak, in this one regard. But it's the most important regard. You can tromp around the woods like a woodsman all you want, shooting the biggest elk that are left, but if you don't fight the outgroup – you're only worth so much.

White people will *kill each other* over 10% on a business deal but they won't fight the outgroup. They'll stare down a grizzly bear and shoot it dead with some expensive, high caliber revolver that gives off Kevin Costner vibes but ask them to face down Communist counter-protestors armed with actual murder weapons and everyone runs for the hills to watch *Duck Dynasty* and do a lazy job of homeschooling their kids. I'm *tough*. I fly-fish just like Brad Pitt in that one movie. The movie that brought me here to the mountains from my suburban Californian s-hole. I drive like a frenzied demon down dirt roads in my loud side-by-side and my wife puts makeup on like Kylie Jenner but we're conservative and I voted for Trump.

That's what it's like around here. That's what conservative tough guys are like. They're *almost* as much a product of the media machine as the liberals. Of course, God and having *somewhat* of a moral spine is the difference maker. And when it all hits the fan, I will happily stand with these people. Until then, I am going to have my say. It's a form of wealthy male conservative vanity. Fight defenseless animals and crush your children down with "discipline" but never, ever – don't you EVER be what the media doesn't want you to be. Be a convenient welcome mat to the Rockies but don't you DARE commit a racism. Don't you *dare* commit an antisemitism. Grow that beard and build them houses but take the jab, consent to the "passport", and switch to EV when Goldman Sachs vultures the last of America's independent energy companies. Take it, white man. You big puss. Hey, you have your dignity though, right? You'll fight *one day*, right? Someday, over the rainbow.

I didn't say much of this to him but I did give him a look that conveyed some it. White guys with status seek to humiliate white guys they perceive to be lower than them. They learned this from the TV. They didn't used to do this before the War of British Aggression (it's a joke, it's a joke, people). The relish he took in that word, "boy". The fobbing me off onto his wife. The expectation I carry him in a certain way. All that is new stuff. He had some of the good old stuff in place. That's why it's not adversarial and probably never will be, between us. He's more me and I'm more him than all these foreigners ever will be. Some people are provoked by the voluminous output here, much of it critical. This is a book. This is what writing lends itself to: cultural criticism. And criticism gets this rap like it's nothing but fault-finding, that there isn't a pot of gold at the end of it. That this isn't to tear down alone but to do a remodel job on a house that badly needs it. We can't just keep dicking around the lakes near Boise and expect the hordes to leave us alone. We can't keep thinking that a salary during Mammon is the measure of a man. We need to get smart. We need to get moving. I'm making the appeals necessary.

Back to the thing I was saying a second ago. White people think they get to mistreat other white people. There's an intimacy and familiarity to people who are closer to you than the outgroup and so you more readily bare your teeth at them. This happens all the time in the home environment. Parents are cover abusers of their children but the moment they're out in public, they seem to grow a moral conscience about parenting. Exceedingly few people spank their kids in public anymore. You used to see a bit of it even in the early 90's. At least I did. People get away with what they think they can get away with. That was a lot of the basis of my critique in *CCC* of this fake business economy. Just because you can sell $100k tiny house villages to people in Oregon, Texas, and Vermont doesn't mean you *should.* We all used to look down on mobile home parks. They were places of last resort. Now everyone has defaulted to last resort because nobody can bring themselves to be just a *bit* confrontational with Democrat operatives. It's all tough talk until the stakes require a *wee* bit of verbal confrontation and suddenly everyone vanishes. But sure, they'll effin' *destroy* each other in business deals and do all sorts of parasitic nonsense. White people are so rotten to each other. Since they are statistically the least ethnocentric of all the races, they do all this covert abuse stuff to one another in their libertarian redoubts. All this does is flood in the cheap labor, lower standards for everyone, and then there's another falling away of territory. The worst perpetrators of this are white liberals, of course. They're the absolute scum of the scum. I get to say this because I'm white. Black conservatives don't get to say this because…haha, I'm not going to say why. You're just going to have to guess. You're just going to have to get further behind the paywall. White liberals have been the death and ruin of us all. Who's the one guy with the 6x6 Biden sign in his front yard in the middle-of-nowhere Idaho? Yeah, he's the one. Who's the condo developer clotting up Bozeman? Yeah, he's the one. Don't get me started on these people. Back to the covert abuse stuff. It's even *more* wrong when you pull a fast one just because you think you can get away with it. This guy thought he could call me "boy" as I'm showing him around my place, even though I'm physically fitter than him and could easily kill him in mortal combat if we were pitted against one another in Da Octagon. Where's the respect? It's the combination of factors, too. Just that one verbal slip could be forgiven or even understood as a term of endearment *but it wasn't*. He was lashing out because he was frustrated that I wasn't falling into place on his social dominance. It is *me* who is dominant. I'm just suave about it because I watched a bunch of old movies and spent a *lot* of time around my Golden Generation grandparents growing up. You don't be underhanded with people. That's a weirdo, neurotic thing that was programmed into us. You deal, straight up. That's the way it works, especially between European bruthas.

People are separated from their instincts by modern media. I want this guy to be more in-charge but he has risen as far as his current operating system will permit. He's capped out. It's too bad. Let there be no confusion: I am not so bothered by his insolence as I am about the entire system of propaganda that turned this guy in a few critical ways against his fellow man. Do not underestimate what a few education units on Martin Luther King Jr. experienced in childhood will do to a person for the rest of their lives.

Don't Let Them Get You Down, King

Young man,

The entire media complex is set against you. Every single thing that has a big budget also has a big agenda. Only a few healthy things have trickled out of the media machine in the last sixty years. You have been lied to about everything. We'll take masculinity, for example. Masculinity is a group endeavor. It is born out of fraternity, patrimony, and conquest. The media has never allowed you to see this. You may not actually know how savory sweet the taste of conquest is, since there has been no conquest in generations. All you have ever been shown is semi-gay action heroes running around, making democracy safe for the world and combatting mildly white ethnocentric, mildly German baddies. Now you just see Michael B. Jordan or Denzel Washington mercilessly slaughtering white men. You've been told that masculinity has to do with accoutrements: fancy ornaments you highlight yourself with in order to impress other men. Masculinity has nothing to do with this. Masculinity has to do with fighting prowess. Sure, you can dress yourself and work out in a way that makes you appear to have fighting prowess. I certainly will not discourage you from that path but you must always place your effectiveness against the outgroup above this. Some of the most masculine men in the world are out of shape and eat terrible diets.

Let's take another example of something you've been wholly lied to about: male and female relationships. When environmental selective pressures were on us and we lived close to death, all was well with men and women. Each had their distinct roles. Man did not think of "permission". He thought of utility and his being enthralled by a woman was the indicator that the breeding pairing was favorable. In other words, man felt immense pleasure when something highly functional was within his grasp. Now women have all these forms of witchcraft granted to them: the Internet, smartphones, caffeine, makeup, surgeries, divorce courts, white knight police forces, intellectual activists in the universities, and so forth. All of these are weapons to use against men, granted to them by bloodsucking overlords who deliberately select *against* goodness and kindness in the human stock. You have to view things from a more Medieval perspective in order to understand the all-out assault currently being perpetrated against white Christian men. Even the word "relationship" suggests apartness. We never lived this way. We lived together in close communion. The concept of a "relationship" is born out of the post-modern age. Men and women once had bliss. They had matrimony. They had union. A "relationship" is a perversion of the language we have casually adopted. The chivalrous approach to women worked for eons and the untold side of it was that men always and forever steered and shepherded women away from evil forces. You can't have the bliss that comes from chivalry if you are not strong enough to shepherd a woman away from the evils in this world. The chivalrous dynamic is so difficult, so distant conceptually that there are few who attain it. The chivalrous, Medieval approach has also been perverted by word-twisters into being a fedora hat, cringe, nerdy thing that only weak men aspire to. Chivalry has *nothing* to do with being munificent with your attentions and adoration. College professors at the highest levels have been eroding what chivalry truly means to the point where all roads lead to fedora hat-tipping cringe. The average condition of virtue of a woman six-hundred years ago compared to today was much higher. The threat of being hacked to death by a sword or strung up for thieving while starving was much higher. The aristocracy of knights and damsels that lent itself to chivalry has been wiped from the earth. All we have is echoes.

There's a whole bunch of other stuff. A random one that comes to mind is South America's deeply European nature. South America was built up solely by European design. South America peaked somewhere in the late 20th Century, before it was robbed by its intellectual elite by mass migration to the United States and before certain neurotic types took control of the immigration bureaucracies in the 1970's and 1980's. As an experiment, track down old pictures of Buenos Aires or Rio de Janeiro. Notice how nicely everyone was dressed. Noticed their demographic makeup. There were entire European-derived cultures in South America that blossomed for the better part of 150 years before being clear-cut by Marxists, completely spoiled and ruined within the space of a single generation. The same can be said about Africa. Watch the

Italian documentary *Africa Addio* to get a small idea of the total scale of the destruction Marxists have brought onto the outposts of European civilization. In particular, pay attention to the bulldozing of the abandoned European estates. Hedgerows carefully managed over the course of decades torn asunder for no reason other than race hatred. Complex interior woodworking hacked away at by hatchets for momentary use as firewood. The patrons murdered in cold blood or driven away by roving guerilla bands. The same has already taken root in America. Think of the splendor and joy for *all* when these estates were thriving. Think of the glorious cultural artifacts born out of that environment.

The soldierly Marxists are all ginned up again. They're probably getting arms and overseas training provided to them before they go back to their apartments and townhomes in the suburbs of major American cities. The glories of the Post War have not been sufficiently erased by the media. Too many who remember correctly still remain and have their own platforms from which to speak. Therefore, a new world war must be devised. Many in my circles are of the opinion that there will be a slow decline. Today, I don't think so. The most elite of the elite don't have the time for that. Ask me tomorrow.

When they were first invented, jungle gyms went twenty feet up into the air. Eventually, someone's dumb kid fell and broke their spine. Now we're at a point where toy manufacturers are only allowed to put caster wheels on *one* set of any device that kids move around in. Decline, everywhere you look. We're all bowling in the bumper lane.

Chin up, king. Don't let them get you down. Changes are coming. Everyone is fed up. *Everyone.* And the evil demons running the show are far less strong than they intimidate you into thinking. We're going to beat them at the ballot box, by golly! I only advocate peaceful solutions. Everything else is *off the table.* Be peaceful and vote for the based candidates that are upcoming. They'll carry us over the finish line! Only do peaceful and legal things. Don't do illegal things. Stay fit. Push back against the lies. Go to meetings. Fight in the culture war. Run for office, please.

The Hits Just Keep Coming

Today I woke up to the news that a black, former NFL pro in South Carolina murdered five white people, including two children and a doctor. Since this act of genocidal terrorism does not fit the media narrative (all white people are evil and shouldn't own guns), the story has already been memory-holed. The children were five and nine years old. They didn't have a chance to enjoy the sweetness of this life. They were snuffed out by a primitive lunatic whose mind was doubtlessly poisoned by the media. This is the reality of America today: we live in a multi-legal system. The left screams about unequal outcomes, that only exist because of IQ differences and not "racism", and then imposes harsher punishments on white people while easing punishment on black people. White people are starting to be murdered, left and right. Seems like every other day a teenaged white girl is being gunned down by a black person. This is not hyperbole, either. Violent crime and murders have skyrocketed since Trump left office.

I am not a legislator. I am not a person with executive position. I cannot tell armed men from the state how to do their jobs and see them follow my suggestions. I can only make an appeal, using my free speech, to the common person out there who takes an interest in what I have to say. I will say this: prepare yourselves for the worst. This is a theme of this book. I set out with this book to keep it light, to have fun, and to be entertaining. That is, after all, part of what I offer: entertainment and content. If I tune into the world *at all*, then the danger assessment kicks in. I am not a paranoid person. I am not guided in my principles from a state of fear. Yet, the growing danger cannot be denied. The foreboding of previous works of mine has turned into themes of crisis management. America is in a state of emergency, to borrow a phrase from Pat Buchanan. Please prepare, while there is still time. The clever take is to say that there is just going to be a gradual decline with no end in sight but remember, America is a much different place from Europe, Canada, or Australia. There has always been the potential for explosiveness here. I am doing my best to defuse the situation but the shot callers in the institutions are ruthless, cynical, and vengeful.

You will want to get to the countryside, as soon as possible. You will want to invest in cryptocurrencies. You will want to team up in preparedness groups. Beware of militias, as they are crawling with Feds. For every veteran who whistle-blows on Fed attempts to turn him against his fellow patriots, there are ten or twenty successful attempts. If you don't know how a person makes their money or their money fundamentals just don't make sense to you, given their lack of quality as value providers, stay the hell away from them. You will want to reckon with the prospect of extremely expensive gasoline prices. You will want to reckon with not being able to shop at the major big box stores because you once upon a time did *something* they can cancel you for. You will want to get your state's legislator guide, print it out, tack it up somewhere it can be seen, and start making phone calls, calmly expressing your concern and what you think reasonable steps to improve the situation would be. You'll want to get off of the centralized food system and have food contacts in your area. If you cannot afford land, you must be willing to be a hungry laborer for someone who owns land. Better to be a serf for a fellow patriot than for one of these demon generals who used tech wealth to buy up land. If you are a young woman, you are going to want to find strong male leader figures to adhere to until you all can find you a suitable pairing. Stop casting yourself into the wind on dating apps. Those don't work anymore and men in America are becoming like self-absorbed pandas: the broodiness has gone out of them. If you are a young man, get a practical skill *yesterday*. Be humble about it. Go to an EMT course. The course doesn't take long and only cost so much. Go to a construction job site and ask for a job, however part-time it has to be. You can't just sit on the computer or your smartphone and watch the world fall apart. You won't make it, that way. You are going to need some kind of value-adding skill that would make a land baron want to take a chance on you. I didn't write these rules. I just observe them coming to the fore. Wage work gives you few essential skills. Branch out. No, being a "Bitcoin investor" isn't good enough. Nobody is going to pay you to sit around the computer in the world that's coming. No one that is moral, that is. Everybody who's worth a damn knows, at this point, to invest in crypto. About the only people left to convince are your Boomer/Gen-X parents, so at least convince them and maybe you'll just live with them for the next however long. Make sure you get your own space though, and that you're treated like a separate adult. You have your own enterprise, even if it's under their roof. And no, video games and "finding yourself" are not enterprises. They are costs. You can pay those costs but only if you bring abundance to the table. A skill is essential.

You do not want to provoke people. You are peaceful! So am I. We just want happy, healthy families for everyone all around the world. We just have a different way of going about it and the most inconvenient part of it is that people have to give up welfare in all its iterations. Despite all the terror stories the media and schools plant in people's heads, the worst of it is that people don't get easy money and have to go get a job and wages rise immediately and there's enough to take care of Abuela and the Down Syndrome cousin. All this fear porn is employed against us. We just want peace. Don't provoke people. I am filled with love and light! It's true. Don't believe the evil ones chopping up my angriest moments out of thousands of hours of content. I chuckle or smile 30 times to the 1 time I scowl and holler. Same goes for you. You're a good person.

You'll want to think about getting a guard dog breed. They're barky, so make sure you can commit to getting them exercise and attention before you make the plunge. You'll want to be armed, of course. You'll want to keep your graceful, service-oriented point of view. We want to serve others. We want to have a good time. Yes, we're getting picked off like flies but we're a happy sort. Together, we are stronger. Every meaningful personal connection you make to another person like you is worth half a million dollars. Don't forget, a lot of people on the other side of the aisle are fed-up too and are more open to appeals than you may think. But don't go seeking them out. Wait until austerity hammers them. Always be proactive and creative and put your own good thing into the world. Let people come to you out of that. I have pointed out the holes in the logic of hippies. Ex-hippies write me emails saying how I helped them out of a dark place. It's a good situation. I don't need to go justify myself to people who don't have my best interests at heart. The ruling elite are a small cadre of hyper evil backstabbers. They don't "cover the spread" well at all. Their reign may be short-lived.

Be careful with wealthy people. As the situation decays, they are going to have more and more say. Careful of the ones who draw paychecks or have extensive interest in the status quo. You will likely *have to* magnetize to wealthy people but choose wisely. Wealthy men have big egos. They don't often respond well to reason and evidence. They want their egos stroked. Men have forgotten the code of conduct of Western capitalism. They run business enterprises differently than they were run in the 1800's, when all of America's real wealth was built up. Beware of wealthy men who are educated. They have been educated the wrong way, guaranteed. They will manipulate you and move you in ways you won't want to be moved but you'll be down in the hole with them, since the country is rapidly falling apart, and you'll just have to go with some of it. And don't be too transient. You'll never find the *perfect* wealthy man to adhere to. Feudalism is here. Wake up, buddy. Wake up, lady. For the young, fertile ladies out there: you will fall into misery and spinsterism if you stick too close to your parents. You would legitimately fair better if you went with a single backpack on your back to some fifty-acre compound in Idaho, Arkansas, Wisconsin, etc. to find a man than hanging around your parents while they fail to attract the labor distribution and collective defenses that the compound is collecting. Sound culty? Newsflash: burning out your fertility with even somewhat conservative parents who don't "get it" is far more culty. There's no Romeo riding in to save you. Most of the breeding stock in America is nerdy, out of shape losers or the smaller fraction of in-shape, greedy predators who are too self-certain and too self-satisfied. The Christ Fire is rare. You're more likely to find it at a compound than wandering around likely a lonely doofus in the suburbs while your parents get overwhelmed by the media and slump into midlife crises. That's just the plain and simple truth. Now be courageous.

Think about raising chickens. There's a nationwide chicken wire shortage. Everyone is thinking about it. Chickens are low startup cost, easy to maintain, disease resistant, amiable and sweet, and give you eggs and then later meat. Their feed-to-food conversion is good. Their footprint is small and you can make good topsoil from their droppings mixed with straw or hay. You can keep them in a little fenced backyard. You can keep them indoors if you have to, like a lot of the Third World does. Chick prices have doubled in the past three years. If you have more than a few acres, or your benefactor does, think about keeping a rooster. Don't be the asshole that drives your neighbors nuts. Raise one if you have the space. Please don't raise geese. They're louder than an elephant and all of your neighbors will secretly resent you. Make friends as you go along.

The country must not be allowed to descend into reeducation camps, holding camps, mass arrests, and judicial persecution of people for having ideas that go against the interests of the system. We're teetering toward these, especially the last one. While you want to get out of the liberal cities, you also want to help others to erect a political bulwark against these cities and their overreach. You cannot simply withdraw, withdraw, withdraw. Yes, you are pulling out of a lot of modernity but you have to build an alternative and you *must* peacefully and legally challenge the existing order. You have to contribute in some fashion to outward pressure from the bastions of sanity left on the globe. You can't just buy Bitcoin and cover your ears and cross your fingers, like a lot of formerly politically active people are doing. Bitcoin can be regulated into a ghetto for a while, at least. Yes, it will burst out of that ghetto. It is a force that cannot fundamentally be contained. But a lot of innocents will get ground up while you wait for the ghetto years to be over. You can always go help Christians protest against lockdowns. You can dine at restaurants owned by patriots and chant "get out" at rapacious health inspectors looking to destroy livelihoods. You can always do something more than transfer money out of fiat. You'll want to get behind people who put nationalism over globalism. Globalism is the path to worldwide genocide, for all peoples. Nationalism is the forward-thinking system that places the interests of the *people* above the interests of the moneyed elite. Find people who will put America First the moment they take office, not international banking interests first (which is what being a Democrat is about). This does not mean you have to be super politically active and take on all the risk in the world. But reward follows risk. You want to have a family and kids but you also have to verbally push back against people like Klaus Schwab, Bill Gates, Anthony Fauci, Joe Biden, and Angela Merkel – who don't want *anyone* to have a family and kids. The more of us that push back by legal means, the more of a future is assured for *everyone*, irrespective of race or creed, to raise a family and kids in peace. Nationalism and decentralization are peace. Globalism and medical overreach are war. Take charge of your personal health. Drop the weight. 80% of COVID patients are obese. Get back to your healthy weight. Everything you do that is positive leads to a decentralized, nationalist world. Everything you do that is immoral and dishonest leads to a centralized, globalist world. Good and evil. Anyway, I said some of this stuff at the end of the last section. I like to end these thoughts on a good note. We can rise above the wave of ultra-violence being unleashed on us.

The West Was Rewritten

She's busy cause she works six days a week and runs a mini farm on the side that she bought with Colorado money. Her kid is sipping a Capri Sun and thumbing at a smartphone. I want to like this lady but she's got curves in the wrong places. She overeats and she's not fresh off a pregnancy. She has the standard two kids that every Millennial who bothers to breed achieves. They all only have two children, deliberately spaced apart by three years. You come to think that this decision is made because it somehow correlates with efficiency in public schooling. Why do public schoolers always do this? No, the explanation has nothing to do with breastfeeding or recovery time. Don't give me that nonsense.

She shakes my wife's hand. Lady, what is wrong with you? She doesn't know better. You have to just tolerate it. You get the clear sense now that she's a liberal but in her quiet thoughts tells herself she's a *Montana liberal*. That means she thinks it's good to keep public lands going so that people can shit it up with dirt bikes or the horses they ride once a year. If you speak out against public lands in Montana, you get in a heap of trouble. Republicans just have to shut their mouths a bit. Democrats prattle on and on about it. Everyone gets to have Montana, right? Just move here and treat it like a public park. We all want to enjoy the natural beauty, equally and democratically. It's *especially* important that greying liberal women over the age of 60 with bad haircuts, Subaru Outbacks they only have serviced at the dealership, and too many cats get to go on their daily or weekly walk using their Indian made walking sticks and quasi-minimalist footwear. These women think they run the roost here. The NPR types. I'd say more but it would be too mean! And the globalist regime *laps up* the prospect of expanding public lands because Klaus Schwab wants nature reserves to fart around on while the rest of the planet starves.

Back to the transplant lady. She leads us to the animal pens. She's got cake butt. Not a pleasant woman to behold because she's got the deceptive glow of sun-kissed skin and she's got good genes but then her eating habits are so bad that you're falsely roped in to checking her out and punished swiftly for the mistake. She's got to quit this job she's working six days a week. You can see the inflammation the stress is causing her: puffy face, puffy cake butt, a mini gut that is creeping toward having its own mind about what direction it moves in. These are the hard years for her. She's putting in work. Where's the man? This is what the man is for. The man busts his body down trying to build up the family's life. Childbirth and nursing are already hard enough on a woman's figure. She's taking on a whole grown man's responsibilities. You hate to see it.

We have a pleasant enough time looking over the livestock. Her father wanders out. He's weak. He's nice as can be but weak. He's not doing the work. He looks pensioned. He has that Boomer ease about him that tells me he's on a retirement system. Agricultural stuff was never his main thing. He dabbled. He may have even done it full-time. But it is not what helped pay for this gaudy craftsman style house and the aggressively overdone shop that this Montana land was carved up for, just a couple years ago. He puts forward the agricultural charm he does with everyone. The up-front face that lets him off the hook. It's pleasant enough. I won't pry. These are staunch anti-racists who hate living around minorities. They're a strange breed. There's too many of them in Montana. They're the main reason I'm unsure that Montana will make it in the long run. Them, the grey ladies, and the out of state real estate developers that seem to get anything they want. Oh yeah, and the invading hordes that will get bussed in when the time comes.

We pick out our livestock and I put the deposit down. They'll be genetic tested so I can register them. I haven't wanted to do that before but for some reason, these days the prospect appeals to me. We'll be back sometime when she's not working. Hard to pin her down. Does she outwork me? I don't think so. But if she did, half the country has been brainwashed to celebrate that and to view her as tougher and more competent than me. Where is the savory joy in this life? Where is the ease of living? It's become a mad scramble and you know you'll just be gunned down for trying to live free, anyway. I won't be running to this woman's farm to help her out. At least there aren't masks on the two kids. The school district is psychotic. I'm sure you're surprised. You'd think in *Montana*, of all places, the school districts would be based – at least some of them. No, we're in big trouble here. The school district hates children with a fiery passion. They're seen as pawns to put in a monthly newsletter *solely* meant to secure levy funds. When the levy is secured, they drop the pretenses and go back to just bullying the kids behind closed doors. You see the graduating classes and they look American but they've been hollowed out. There's a special kind of hatred that liberals have for these further flung, rural communities. They're extra rapacious when they get their hooks in. You experience it like the shock of seeing a beautiful painting be paint-bucketed by some topless activist. And the people here just take it. They're all Netflix and Amazon dependents. But the reaction is building. There's good people here. They are in a race against time they don't understand. The intelligence swamp understands it all too well. Rural people don't know the kind of intellectual and verbal sophistication they need to bring to the chessboard. They've been sincere their whole lives. When some transplant from Colorado comes in and shits up the schoolboard, they think they can deal with this demon in a sincere and disarming way. A lot of them are used to being preached to in this fashion. They think that if they can just get to the *heart* of the Colorado transplant, they'll be able to help this fellow human being see the error of their ways. They disregard the violence that was already done to the precious Montana environment just for this person to have somewhere to park their crossover SUV. They think that these transplants are like that main female lead in *Field Of Dreams*. That even though she's a liberal, anti-racist, she still has a heart and soul and wants to support her man doing his thing. That movie is so hateful. It's like *Dead Poets Society*, beautifully done at the highest levels with a rotten message in its core. The seizure of true Americana followed by subtle changes to the script here and there is at the heart of what has happened to the American West.

I take no pleasure in this. I'm here to transact, out of necessity. This isn't an old American way. This is strange and unsettling but I need to get it done. You can't unconvince millions of people anymore. They shut down the only path to doing that, namely Facebook, YouTube, and Twitter. People's decision-making pathways are lined in blood. Blood is running. You want to stop it. You want to cry out. I think of that Sam Roberts line, "It gets so hard that a stone would cry out." People won't deprive themselves of their little comforts and so they will be deprived by an outside force. They have chosen technological overlords to do that to them. They will go the hard way. All of this here is looking to go the hard way. I know a better way. I know the way out of madness. I know the Lonesome Valley. Nobody wants to walk it, anymore. They want to crystalize and adhere to what the television told them. The tide will come and wash it away. We try for higher ground but we are not billionaires.

Years ago, I had a nicely fleshed out concept for a novel that came to me in a dream. I was shopping at a syndicate grocery store on the compound. I was somewhere within three hours driving distance of Salt Lake City's Temple Square. You had to use food vouchers that were based off of your labor hours.

Control Through Shame

Controlling others through shame is a tricky one. On the one hand, I do not believe in it and do not practice it, especially in my personal life. On the other hand, something akin to shaming does indeed work[2]. There is a whole arsenal of psychological weapons that power-seeking and power-holding people employ. You have to contend with them, even it is just to undo their power. You have to develop thick skin in order to deal with them and you have to be able to dish it back out to them. Evil people do not get dislodged from power magically by libertarian theories. They get dislodged by adversaries. Those adversaries may employ control through shame. I won't get in their way.

Let's talk about our personal lives, then, and leave the statecraft aside for another day or for someone more competent than I to speak on the subject. Controlling others through shame runs the gamut of behaviors. Most commonly, it is holding people to standards they do not understand or are not good standards in and of themselves. When you hold someone to a standard, and it is healthy, you want to be sure that people in your personal life understand the *why* of the standard. Where does it come from?

---

[2] https://www.breitbart.com/social-justice/2016/07/05/fat-shaming-is-good-science/

What purpose does it serve? How can you explain it through, start to finish? If a person does not understand, they will be confused by your influence on them. Clarity in communication is key to not provoking shame in others. If you are holding someone to an unhealthy standard or to a standard that is *somewhat* healthy but not parsed out, a person cannot coherently self-reflect with a methodology where suppositions, temptations, trespasses, and alternatives are fully processed with the standard in mind. "Don't do drugs" is positing a standard and it's a healthy one but without the reasoning behind the standard explained, a person more or less has to default to obedience – especially if he's a child and has little to no life experience. It is so incredibly important that people be helped to understand the *why* of *all* standards we are pronouncing. The imposition of standards without that crucial care and understanding will store up as resentment in a person, and shame because they have an inferior sense about themselves that they cannot fully explain, and eventually rebellion will show up in the person's behavior.

Rebellion is extremely tricky territory because it is a part of the human experience to go through *some* measure of rebellion in early adulthood. The less that moral standards were explained to a person in childhood, the more room there is to work with the Devil has in positing *new* moral standards with fully fleshed out explanations when that person rebels. The Left knows precisely when a person is most vulnerable to breaking from the teaching of their parents, early adulthood, and has knowingly taken over all of the universities in the West to take full advantage. The results have been ruinous. Not only is the New Age morality being taught in the universities, it is also being pushed in corporate work places, hospitals, civil service, the military, and all other non-small business avenues of employment.

We can never fully erase rebellion. We don't have to. We simply have to know what healthy rebellion looks like. It looks like Jesus going off into the desert, being offered a kingdom of Earthly pleasures, and deciding to continue on the true path. We will all be tempted. We will all get distance from our parents, as part of a healthy maturation process. We need to be able to define ourselves, even if it's just nights and weekends while we work the family business in the day. Rebellion keeps us fresh. The old guard does not so readily give up its throne. We need the tide to ebb and flow.

Controlling others through shame in our personal lives is valid if a person has fallen to evil-doing, especially when explaining standards all the way through has little or no effect. You don't want to get in the habit of doing this, though, because you have to ask yourself why you have an evil-doer in your life in the first place. With business, we can't really help it because the world is filled with people under demonic possession. You are public-facing and the public is insane. But in your personal life, you want to be as proactive as possible. Through your expression, you want to repel evil people as far away as possible (to the point where they choke off and starve out in the void), and you want to compel morally excellent people toward you. A quick "control through shame job" on a person in your personal life is a once in a blue moon kind of thing. You do *not* want your role in this life to be one of stopping metaphorical drunk drivers from making mistakes, over and over again. If you have friends who keep getting into trouble, they are a reflection of you. If you have family members who keep getting into trouble, one of their parents did that to them and you have to work with the source some. You can't just be herding cats, to use a Boomer turn of phrase.

People are generally intellectually developed to some extent but their emotional development is somewhere near what mass media has programmed them to be: dependent, tattle tale babies who soil themselves and need Big Government to rescue them from their unending misery. You don't want to spend much of your gifts tangling with people like this. This is why I keep a wide, wide berth from controlling others with shame. It's not that I think it's completely invalid. There are cases where you have to use it, especially in self-defense. You simply need to think about what using this level of awareness does. You have thrown chum in the water with a bunch of circling sharks. You do *not* want to care more about people's lives than they care about their own. You want to associate with people who *can* reason their way through things, understand consequences for bad behavior from a mile away, and who can self-regulate in the times they misstep. This is a lot to ask for in today's day and age but if you persevere and stay true to yourself long enough, good people will filter through to you.

The approximate opposite of control-through-shame is influence-through-encouragement. You want to provoke in people their moral courage. People respond well to inspired people. For as sorry a state as most of humanity is in, if you accurately depict the good vs. evil dimension in all things when you speak – most people want to do good and will adjust accordingly. The Left knows this and so they depict climate change as the evil and mass personal sacrifice in living standards as the good that will cure the evil. True believers on the left feel *really good* about themselves, in their own minds, even though to healthy people they look like demonic imps. Every bit of scientific data, journalist integrity, hour of television, and direct CIA programming through yoga classes or improv groups or whatever has told them that they are with the right cause. They are on the right side of history! Sports leagues affirm this. Banks affirm this. They just have to keep going. Keep growing! All of this stuff is gradually undone, by reality itself not conforming to their "science", but also at a faster clip by truthtellers who have a clearer framing on the *real* good vs. evil playing out in the world: billionaire pedophiles vs. literally everyone else but especially America's white middle class. Billionaires, of course, have unending resources to expend against genuine truthtellers. They especially attack truthtellers who factor in race to geopolitics in an accurate way. People who over-factor race receive billionaire funding and intelligence agency employment. People who under-factor race receive billionaire funding and get TV shows on Fox and CNN…and intelligence agency employment. Few prominent voices affirm this worldview of good vs. evil. You will be deliberately cut out of corporate, governmental, non-profit, and international employment if you demonstrate any kind of sympathy to this worldview. Life will be very difficult for you even if you do get the jab and allow yourself onto the track-and-trace grid that is being built by Microsoft and SalesForce.

The left controls through shame, all the time. They tell you you're bad because of the color of skin you were born with. They skip straight over the actual crime statistics broken down by race and go straight to outliers of extreme violence committed by white people and say that everyone who is white and ethnocentric is essentially culpable of those acts of extreme violence. They scream at mothers who won't wear masks. Using Capitol Police, they beat the living snot out of Trump supporters. They ritualistically humiliate white champions by pitting them into bad match-ups while giving nothing but favorable match-ups for black champions. The hardest of roads is always laid out for the white guy who wants to do anything notable with his life, all because the color of his skin. The left also shames the living hell out of blacks who defect from media programming and choose to be conservative or just in simple favor of smaller government. The left does not seem to do much in the way of shaming Jewish conservatives, which is really interesting to note. There's only one of those they ever go after. The left puts children in camps, puts embarrassing masks on them, puts them in plastic dividers when they go to school, shoots them full of gene therapy drugs, chemically castrates them, hormonally rewires them, and all manner of other things that induce shame in a person because they are no longer living in a way that roots them to natural morality.

Influencing others through encouragement means showing them the true nature of what evildoers are up to, how they have taken near complete control of the moral narrative at the heart of civilization (through mass indoctrination), and how people can fight back against the rising tide of world revolution. But it can also be as simple as celebrating little victories a younger person achieves. Or giving someone support as they step out of their comfort zone and assert the truth in a way they hadn't before. Or in providing moral instruction to someone who wants to be better about managing their personal affairs. You don't have to flare out into the grand scheme of things. Encouragement can boil down to a few words of support. Over time, if you live to encourage others, you will find that people look to you for influence when times are tough. This is a natural responsibility that we commonly took on, simply as a matter of living in a non-central banking, non-welfare world. People had station because they were good at helping others through difficulties. There was a moral order. Now, because morality has been inverted through mass media programming, those who are the best at covertly killing large numbers of people or sickening people's minds and ruining their decision-making abilities are the ones who hold the most station. They get the most honorary doctorates. The state redirects resources to them. They have strange meetings on yachts out in the middle of the ocean and then go back to their estates and engage in new rounds of political activism. They go on TV shows and audiences treat them like total charmers, even if their personalities suck or have soured. They're just so charming and funny! They tell the most provocative and disarming stories! What a laugh. They decide which uniformed troops kill which civilians. Every single person you see promoted by corporations and mass media has done something gravely evil in their lives, even if it is just the compounding effect of their verbal manipulation over time. You can have been an actor for thirty years, starred in nothing but turkeyburger movies that soften people up to the notion of worldwide government and the dissolution of the family, and be rightfully considered one of the evilest people alive. You only get in the club if you do evil things.

Let's take an actionable example of this shame vs. encouragement thing. Say you have a friend who wants to "find himself". He displays artistic sensibilities. He's a *little* too open with the world and gets bogged down in either depression or flights of fancy or both. This causes him to be an unreliable worker. He can't hold down a job. He can't build up his enterprise. He flounders. He retreats into isolation because he doesn't feel good about this. Do you hammer him for it? Maybe he *does* need someone to be tough with him and snap him out of it. But do you use *shame*? Do you mess with his self-concept, injecting negative ideas about himself in there, and then not fully explain things out so he's left just kind of...infected by you? Sounds like a jab, huh? Sounds invasive. Sounds like an entire multi-trillion-dollar system of control runs off of this very principle. Of course, you don't treat this guy this way. You point out how he's doing some things well and has self-defeating habits built up in other ways, if you do it at all. You give perspective with a *balance*. That way, the young fella's agency is always kept in mind and the real hope of improvement is within his grasp. You never leave a person in their own darkness, if they're *sincerely* coming to you for help. You always show the balance, even if things are dire, so that evil and dysfunction can reasonably be overcome. People who flay truth-seeking others with their own inadequacies aren't behaving aristocratically, they're just dicks to their own people. But people who flay evil-doing globalists with their own inadequacies *are* behaving aristocratically. And the more artfully and intelligently they do it, the more effective they are at arresting and disintegrating the murder march of climate justice, social justice, and whatever other bloodlust they tack "justice" to the end of.

Weak liberals confuse severity with shaming. They think that since someone is working to contain their evil-doing in a serious fashion that their true self is under attack. This is not true. It is their false self that is under attack. It is the festering cancer of propaganda being excised from their bodies that is causing them pain and shame as it struggles to keep its tentacles wormed into the host. The more a person is objectively morally good, the less they are bothered by someone thundering on about moral things. The intelligence services know this and so they have deliberately programmed Marxist operatives to reframe the unpleasantness that comes from mind parasites being dislodged from their systems as further evidence that the good person is in fact failing at cultural competencies, multiethnic awareness, is demonstrating antiquated patriarchal bigotries, or some other lack of sensitivity. This is a second layer of psychological defense that is programmed into the average Marxist activist. Since this second layer of counter-reactivity can be beaten by more dedicated truthtellers, there is a third layer of psychological defense that the intelligence agencies put into their activists. This is the "body energy certainty" level. Marxist programming pulls from Third World folkish sensibilities in order to put a third line of defense against uncertainty and deprogramming. Basically, the intelligence services try to tie globalist propaganda to people's already existing "blood memories". The Mossad figured this out a long time ago with their "Return" passages to the Holy Land. They work at something deep within a person: their ancestral memories. They weave and weave the struggle for global revolution into these deep senses in a person, through long, long hours of training exposure. This can be achieved in a classroom with Powerpoint presentations but it is the Marxist operatives who go "back to Africa" and have their "Ali, bumaye!" moments that are the ones who get the third line fully put into place. This is a lot trickier of a level of programming to defeat because then the truthteller has to have clarity on their own blood memories. In fact, they have to have *more* clarity on their blood memories and perhaps even tap into something deeper – which I'll get into another time – that can dislodge the *body certainty* of the Marxist activist. The top brass of Black Lives Matters gets this training. High level actors get this kind of training. Bankers and lawyers at the highest levels get this third level training. You have to have a deeper sense of self than they do and they've been fostered by Adorno, Reich, and intelligence agencies refining these methods for two generations. What do you have? Well, you may have a lot but you still have to step inside their third level of certainty and undo the framing of the psychic energy running through their physical core, from their lower shoulders down into their lower guts. And you have to do this in a relatively quick amount of time before they figure out what you're doing to them. The highest-level ones have agents they have internalized that are on the lookout for this thing. The Deep State was so cocky and fucking stupid when they released *Inception*. It's all a metaphor for MKULTRA, magik, and freemasonry. They literally do inception on people in underground labs. They do it to the highest value assets to the cause of the breakaway civilization. How do you, as the average person reading my book, contend with this? You have to reach far, far back in time to when their methods weren't as refined and they didn't dictate so much of world consciousness. They play the stock market as well as they do because they have been trained in the occult. They know how people at the shallower levels of awareness/cognition/depth operate. They have the power to hold everyone less initiated than them in a thrall. George Soros is not a collection of bad arguments. He has had extensive programming training and there are exceedingly few people above him, in terms of magik. The left is so dumb though because they put all of this stuff in readily visible places, figuring that they will always and forever be able to drown high level truthtellers in the labyrinth of complexity they have set forth. You see this with people who go into the occult, hoping to undo it all and blow the whistle and set everyone free. They always get felled at a certain level. But you don't need to go into all that. Simply stay anchored to God. Live true! Stay sober. Stay clean. Hold on to your innocence, even when they turn up the psychic attacks to full blast. Hold fast. And flex on them. They're weak. They're just extremely sophisticated and hyper high IQ. That's no substitute for goodness or love. Stupid dummies, they openly broadcast how they reprogram people because they figure no one alive anymore is sophisticated enough to simply reverse engineer the process. Hubris. Pure hubris.

Every sincere artist puts out stuff that helps you come out from under the spell. Take all the good stuff that patriots are doing and centrifuge it, like the vaccine makers do. Isolate the best bits. Centrifuge those again. Drink it in, like honey mead or kefir. Go back to your Christian patriots. Imbibe. Get those muscles nice and red. Get thick. Honky-tonk. Go into the blood. Remember the old, old ways. Talk with your elders. If they're dead and gone, remember their sense of life. Let it pass through you and fill up all your pores. Document it and put it on your walls, so you're reminded. Do not gaze into portals for too long. Look away from the computer screen. Break your eyes away *constantly* from the television screen. Shield the children's eyes, for the love of God. People have TV Brain. Do not listen to them. Look for the old sensibilities, always. Hone in. Robots are here to kill us all. Debit card swiping pads put psychic cancer into your hands. Endure the power lines and the wi-fi. It won't always be this way. Do not fixate on the clowns they parade before you. Don't be a Boomer like that. Focus on the long conversations. Focus on the breath going into your lungs. Be a real human being. Protect the king. Fight for the king. The king rules. Try to embody the king. Retrain your body. Be musky. Be the bear in the cave and amble out in the spring. Understand that every new show is CIA programming. Every new movie is CIA programming. They control all of it. Rub dirt between your hands. Put your bare feet on the ground and feel the electromagnetic healing. Remember anthems and war chants. Plunge into ice *but do NOT* allow a guru to soothe-speak to you immediately thereafter. Get away from the productivity psychonauts. Stay away from the psychedelic users. The MMA fighters I mentioned earlier in the book are avatars of social control, fighting in a peanut gallery of the mind. They are not real. Patriots are real. Angels are real. Find your guardian angel. Pick one of the saints. Let him protect you and un-incept you from the burrows and mazes the Blood Killers have cast down us all like a net. Let's flippin' go, king. Awaken! Come out of the shackles. Break them! Truly break them! Onward to Christ. Onward to nature. Onward to clean water and clean air. Push back. Step up. Take it like a man and keep coming. Conquer.

Listless In The Home

Everybody is back to living with their parents. The world is shutting down. I get it. The financial realities of decades of free stuff are coming home to roost. Upward mobility is shot. There's no point in participating in the modern economy since there's no freedom. You resort to speculation or you just wait around, at home, with your parents, hoping that things will blow over. This, of course, is *bad* for your health.

To some extent, your parents were complicit in this mess. Democrat Boomers are the most complicit. Followed by state employees. Followed by Big Business, cheap labor folks. On and on. You'll just have to gauge for yourself. Some people were not complicit at all but they're like 2% of the people aged 50 and older. We won't label these people, out of respect for their anonymity and because they paid their dues.

When you're at home, listless, waiting for "happenings" and economically disabled, your personality starts to bump into the ceiling of your parents' personality limits. Maybe it's an intellectual thing and you were born smarter than them. More commonly it is because you know the arguments better, have been far less compromised or corrupted for far less time, and because they know have to live with the limits they set upon themselves as moral agents during their prime productive years. I am not saying it's too late for anyone's parents. I'm simply pointing out that our decisions from decades ago *do* accrue to us. And remember, I'm talking about what is roughly a First World Problem here. Being relegated to living as a NEET with your parents while the world falls apart is not the absolute worst position to be in, in this life. But here you are, waiting for another day to pass while your dominant, nervous, breadwinning parents live a fuller life than you, because of their enfranchisement to this sick system, while you check social media and wait for the situation to improve.

You will have to break out of this. To do this, you have to come out from under this depressive spell your parents are keeping you under. They want you nearby. They want you safe. They will need you to take care of them in the future. You're scared to leave! You're scared your poor mother will croak from her frail health or because your dad is overweight and a pandemic is going on. Or maybe you have younger siblings you feel beholden to. Or a niece. Or a younger cousin. The Family Card is a powerful card to keep you hanging out in your childhood room, glued to the Internet, remaining somewhat oblivious of what the exact expense is to keep you every month, and wishing on a star that things were different.

Another card is the Economy Is Shot card. This is a persuasive one. Why take a job with Chipotle when they're going to shove plastic nubs up your ass and expose you to nauseating levels of The Eagles on the house sound system? Why go to university when the professor is going to pound you in the face with Marxism and everyone is dead inside? You don't want to wade out into that.

Maybe you trade a little crypto or something. A lot of dudes are "day traders". That usually means they put their stimulus checks into crypto and ride the current wave upwards. There's nothing wrong with this. It's just kind of a no-brainer. Maybe, probably, everyone should be doing this. It's a more honest living than being a rapaciously greedy tiny home developer or whatever, I don't care. Stupid economy. Buy crypto, folks.

None of this is fulfilling and your parents' disillusionment and escapism hovers above it all. Their house, their tone. This is an immovable rule of living in the world. You can have all the best ideas but you are still limited by your landlord. Property tax is just the government being everybody's landlord. We are all caged animals, to one degree or another. Every single person in the United States. It's making us miserable. Living with your parents may be making you miserable. It probably is. That doesn't automatically mean they're bad people. You may even enjoy each other's company on a regular basis. Things may be relatively peachy but it's not the same as living on your own. Irrespective of the enjoyment, you *will* bump into the ceiling of your parents' personality development. There's a roof over you and it is psychic. Your dad just isn't as into your life as you are. Your mom may be *too* into your life. There's a miscalibration somewhere that is born out of years upon years of bad habits. Otherwise, why would you be living at home in these times? The Trump years were so prosperous. Any adult over the age of 18 or 19 coming out of the Trump years with *responsible* parents would be positioned to move out. That won't be the case in a couple years when people's teeth start falling out of their heads because the federal government is carpet bombing what little bit of America's riches is left. Financial conditions aside, living with your parents is stifling! There's not even a need to decide whether your parents prepared you adequately or not. The fact is, you're living with them and you'll want to move out, eventually. As I wrote in *MSKGA*, try this stuff out as suggestions. I'm not big into edicts. You don't know me! I don't know you. In these books, it's all meant to provoke thought.

To weather living with your parents during the United Nations' attempt at complete global totalitarianism, you have to be willing to push your parents away a bit. Not to be "alienated" from them, as the leftists would want you to do. To differentiate and get your own thing going, as any reasonably entrepreneurial parent would encourage their child to do. Lots of people are caught up in this situation and their parents are not reasonably entrepreneurial. Living with state employee parents during the lockdowns is like having your soul locked down. You have to bust out of that, some. "But Steve! My dad is a firefighter and my mom is a teacher," is the retort. "They're essential workers!" Yeah, okay. You're getting HR trainings filtered through to you by these people who operate in state cartels that basically are impossible to enter into unless you're a jabber who's benefitting from the trillions the Fed is dumping into the states. There's a price to this. The price gets passed on to you. Poop rolls downhill.

You've got to tend to your mind, like a garden. Don't get sick off of checking the Internet, expending your serotonin in an effort to take the edge off of how bored and uninspired you feel and how being around your parents sometimes feels like just an extension of that. It's not easy to maintain a car when premiums are going up, because the country is being openly invaded by a hostile force, and the gas is expensive because globalists don't like fracking. You should try, though. You should try to get out of the house. Maybe you'll live with friends. Maybe you will live inawoods. You don't *have* to move out but would it make you happier? You have to foster your own development, not do "roommates" with your parents. That said, it's not the height of evil to live with your parents when the true unemployment percentage is higher than a homerun hitter's batting average. No need to get down on yourself. We're just talking about that experience of hitting the grey ceiling of your parents' limits as people and how in previous times, you could readily do something about it. We're in emotional food stamps world and we're figuring out how you can rig things so that you still stand up and getting moving on your own steam. People are getting fired for any politics right of center. Everything in the work sphere is low T and low energy. Still, you've got to *dance*, brothers and sisters. You've got to move those feet. You've got to beat the odds. Stay away from student loans, unless you're going to beat them through inflation and crypto gains, and get dancing. Get your hustle going, player. Don't allow yourself to be limited by the domesticating tendencies of your parents, who have a 99% chance of being more enfranchised and better off than you. There's no such thing as free. You ain't getting free rent. There's strings attached, especially the less self-knowledgeable your parents are. Emphasis on *especially*. If you have a brother living over the garage, what's his fulfillment in this life? Is he meeting his potential? Is he frustrated? Does he mull over joining the military from time to time? Yes, all males are going through some version of this, but does the free rent contribute to that? Emotional subsidies are tough because I can't just say, "Go flip burgers like I did when I was your age!" You will get your face punched in by a...haha, by a youth! *Something* has to happen, though. Maybe you have to go a little insane to break out of the ennui. Maybe you have to pounce on the first chance you get, the first hand that extends your way to help you out of your parents' place. Maybe you have to write emails to people you can think of and ask if they know of anything. Just don't choose uninspired people. You *may* be better off living in a closet, pissing in a bottle at night, over a business space that's closed at night downstairs below you, than living with your parents over their garage. Necessity is both perceivable as a mediating force to external circumstances but also something you ruffle up inside of yourself to overcome the greyness.

Isolation

Nowadays there is every reward for isolating yourself and every punishment for going and connecting with like-minded individuals. You are given bribes by the government to stay home. You are made glowing promises and given special medical attention just for laying about. In terms of punishment, you are hunted by intelligence agencies, screamed at and sometimes beaten by activists who are making a lot more money than you to take to the streets. You are tracked by bloodsucking corporations, badgered to wear a mask by insane people, given stinging traffic tickets while the country is being invaded with the explicit support of the US military, and treated like you're evil if you go have a snowball fight in the park.

One of the pernicious aspects of social isolation is self-absorption. An overconcern with the self develops. It manifests like hypochondria, where you are overaffected by every little thing. Maybe you're too concerned with sound. Or you can't get enough media in you, no matter how you try. Or you get overweight and then blame your social paralysis on being overweight. You tell too many stories about yourself. You spend too much time indoors and develop a Vitamin D deficiency and then you get sick and feel relieved that you're sick and have something to blame your woes on. You think you're far more interesting than you actually are and exhibit "I am very special" moments when you do socialize. Your latent talents and skills you formerly developed go to waste and you tell yourself over and over that one day you will retake your former glory but nothing happens and the months slide by (years now, with the globalist medical scam that's running). Self-absorption also shows up when you can't gauge another person's interest in what you're saying. You have been stewing in your own thoughts and maybe, probably they're not even that compelling. Talking about what's going on in the world *currently* is a way of getting around that, but you still may not say it in an interesting or engaging way. There is a craft to socializing that comes from long hours of spending time in meaningful conversation in a group or pair setting. You need fresh input. We all do!

Most of the beautiful works of art, infrastructure, architecture, and all the beauty in culture come from many people, of similar background, working harmoniously in the direction of goodness. Now and then there are rare geniuses who catalyze beauty on their own but even they are the products of strong, fervent cultures.

In youth, a person needs roads that lead back to themselves so they can define who they really are. This happens from about age 13 to age 23. Some people miss the boat on this and have to go further into their 20's finding themselves. This is not ideal, whatsoever. The roads that lead back to oneself have to be pivoted to lead outwards to others, once one has found oneself. The effect of totalitarian governments shutting down business and forcing people into the home has been to ratchet up isolation and strongarm people into becoming self-absorbed. In countries where SSRI and welfare usage are high, the populace is relatively untroubled and many even celebrate being relieved of social responsibility. Socialists always and forever want to escape back into the womb, where everything was warm and they felt safe and every physical need was taken care of by a tube. To persist as a liberal in the modern age is to be profoundly emotionally immature.

Lots of people who intellectually identify as conservative, libertarian, minarchist, monarchist, pro-freedom, anarcho-capitalist, or some variation of wanting to reduce the size and scope of the state have emotionally immature tendencies. The most sophisticated organizers and financiers on the Left understand that keeping people emotionally and spiritually immature is *essential* to their continued success. For every "redneck" out there who defines himself as a whiskey-drinking Denver Broncos fan with a big truck and don't give a ____, there's a Democrat voter who slips onto the rolls unnoticed and unaccounted for. Self-absorption is a way of being in an emotional ghetto where media and false identities keep a person nicely sated and disabled as political opposition. "MAGA" was a nice emotional comfort blanket for a lot of people who thought that by electing one single person, everything would be made better again. A lot more people are waking up to the fact that they've got to *do something*. Complaining on social media worked for about two years until Big Tech just censored anyone inconvenient. Complaining is an easy out for people who develop a hypochondriac condition with respect to socialism. "Oh, I don't like the city council doing this. Glad I'm getting social media points for bellyaching about it. This is a proxy for the care and attention I should have gotten when I was a child. I'm immature!" That's about the gist of it.

The world is in *big* trouble. Just today the news came out that 100 top corporate executives across the United States working for the airlines, media, law, and investment held a meeting about what they're going to do to combat states changing their voter laws to make it harder for the globalists to cheat. That's some serious brain power coming together. The combined net worth of those people is easily over $10 billion. Those people came out of isolation to brainstorm and game plan. They experienced social benefits such as elevated mood, a sense of empowerment, the lifting of depression, and self-expression. They're doing it in this evil way but nonetheless, they got to have an experience that maybe you didn't in the past week or month or however long you've been cooped up.

The world is yours for the taking. You just have to leave your room and do something that involves adding value to the life of other human beings. Maybe it starts with going to church. Maybe you go to the gym. You'll want to be real about what matters. There may be precious little time to convey these things to anyone willing to listen. The *real human beings* are yearning for others to join their ranks. Interacting for longer periods of time, stomaching discomfort, working to be more of a leader so that you don't slump into discomfort and awkwardness, and coming up with some *purpose* to it all is what you have to do to get out of self-absorption. You are not going to navel-gaze or meditate your way out of self-absorption. Some people need to meditate a little bit to calm down or get a bit of insight. That's not a big deal unless they over-calibrate and put too much stock in their self-concern. The world is falling apart. You have to be strident and conquer. Take possession of as much of the social and economic atmosphere as possible or someone else will.

Yellowstone and Group Strategy

I just wrapped up watching the first season of *Yellowstone*, starring Kevin Costner and a bunch of Millennials. It's turning ghey pretty fast but there are flashes of promise in it, like maybe they'll steer the show conservative a bit. All the baddies are liberals. If you haven't watched the show, you're not necessarily missing out on much. They fetishize Montana a lot and try for beautiful vistas above any substantive quality the show has on a philosophical level. The overriding message is indeed sympathetic to generational Montanans fighting back against their state getting utterly ruined by clueless Californians but there's that heavy bit in it that any tourism board would approve of.

The main character is John Dutton. He's played by Kevin Costner, who still looks good in his old age. His voice has become comically gravely but it's affable and Kevin has only improved as an actor as he's aged, despite Hollywood misusing him for the better part of two decades. John Dutton has a mega gigantic ranch that's been in his family for 130 years or something like this. A greedy Indian and a butt-wipe Californian real estate developer want to steal his land and destroy him. On top of that, Dutton wasn't a very good father to his four children and they're all messed up pretty badly. His wife is long gone. He's managed to accrue a tremendous amount of political control in Park County and in

Montana in general. He's losing his power because the state is turning fake and gay because of liberals moving in and destroying everything, like they always do. The show never states this explicitly because the real estate lobby in Montana would ax the show, if Hollywood didn't beat them to it, but the dynamic is undeniable.

John Dutton is depicted as running a semi-criminal enterprise. His daughter is a corporate hatchet man with an amazing body. His son is a shark lawyer who smooths over legal issues that arise with the ranch. His oldest son is an incel cowboy who never leaves the ranch. His youngest son is a crybaby soldier who married a feminist squaw and lives on the reservation with a single, neglected boy. John Dutton's righthand man is a terminator cowboy killer who does plenty of dirty work whenever John asks. Everyone has done something bad yet for the forces of evil that have gathered around them, you do sympathize with their plight to some extent. They are set up against people more evil and conniving. And Dutton's moral center is to keep the ranch intact to be able to pass it down. None of his messed-up children even want the ranch or have the slightest interest in fertility.

The show's fundamental premise is flawed because no one who acquired that much power and influence in a rural area in America would neglect to raise their children to see the value in having children. Every one of John Dutton's children are self-concerned genetic dead-ends. The daughter is far too mannish. The lawyer son is played by Wes Bentley, who has made a career off of playing the fop. The youngest son is totally whipped by his low IQ wife. Maybe the characters will be remediated by season three. The whole spectacle is sad and the show offers little levity. Oh, and there's black cowboys everywhere, for some reason. The show plays a bit like the inside of Kevin Costner's psyche: a mildly left leaning Midwesterner who decided to play the cowboy and now has no one to pass his legacy on to. I doubt the show would have been greenlit if the main character had been firmly conservative and lived by precept so essential like...I don't know, *having his children have more children themselves.*

This is a huge theme in America. Older people are having to come to terms with America becoming significantly worse, with an undeniable liberal, Third World flavor, because they spent their formative years on acquisitive behavior instead of investing in people. Millennials are the worst generation in American history, even worse than Gen-X. Not by much, but by a bit! They don't have children. They organize for all the wrong things. They accept *fun*employment instead of fighting for real work. They are so badly damaged by media that they think adults in the Northeast in business suits should make all the difficult decisions in society. They think *important things* are decided at the UN and Davos. They spaz out over medical tyranny hustlers. Millennials are just broken. The few good ones took for the hills, long ago. Boomers are culpable for their atrocious parenting styles and they have saddled us all with legions of irremediable, concrete-solid narcissists who want to wipe the white race from the face of the planet. What a dump America is becoming. Older people see this and are troubled by it but don't have the thrust to change it, anymore. They feel relief when some Millennial staffer for a think tank comes along and acts confident and proposes solutions. There's really only about 20,000 people left in America who can actually fix the situation, with *everyone* pitching in of course, and these people have been cajoled into digital gulags so the word can't get out. It's not check-mate time though because the ruling regime is overreaching way too fast, disrespecting and persecuting conservatives to a lunatic degree, and the economic catastrophes now unfolding are waking *lots and lots* of people to the peril before them.

Hopefully there's a wake-up call in *Yellowstone* that brings the Millennials back to sanity. John Dutton is depicted as such a meanie when someone threatens the core of his moral compass, the sanctity of the ranch. Ooh, he's so mean when he tells his kids to buck the f up, to steel themselves and find the resolve. Yet, this is what it takes when you have a badly compromised situation you have to come back from. Yes, his parenting sucked. Yes, he overinvested in acquisition and underinvested in fertility. But these things can't be easily changed. The citadel remains. The throne remains. The people are few but the place they get to gather is still intact. The neurotic, self-loathing wreckage that drifts around in the form of Millennial screw-ups still needs to surmount one last titanic effort if the citadel is to be saved. We'll see how the show goes. I'm in for one more season. I really can't stand the feminist squaw or the writers pumping feminism as hard as they are. Feminism is failing, badly, and few are making excuses for it.

Maybe that changes in the course of the show, since the episodes I just watched are a few years old now.

Single family homes are being bought up by the pension funds of Canada, Singapore, Germany, and a couple other countries. Chinese are dumping all their funny money into American real estate. Wall Street wants to play landlord. Millennials are getting hyper-boned on real estate and they don't care much. But some are starting to care. There's hope, still. There are a lot of people and conglomerates "owning" things in America that don't belong to them. The media is working overtime to hide this fact. It won't hold. The tide is turning, big league.

I should talk about group strategy for a bit. If you view the Yellowstone Ranch as an enterprise and not a family outfit, some things fall into place differently. Kevin Costner has been pitted with a bunch of Millennial actors and only a couple are really up to his caliber, Cole Hauser as Rip Wheeler and Kelly Reilly as Beth Dutton. These are not his children. They're actors and they have to keep the Western film genre alive somehow. The Western suffers from modernist intrusions, like women in men's bunkhouses, blacks awkwardly shoehorned in to everything, women having to unnaturally attempt to be men, asshole lawyers mucking everything up, and Indians sick off of race theory thinking they're somehow aggrieved. The easy peace between men and women is gone. The danger is no longer from the elements but from effed up liberal writers thinking they know how things work. Lawyers, lawyers, lawyers. Kevin Costner has to keep the flame going but there are these troubles in the way. It takes a group strategy to win.

It takes men acting like men, which sometimes means they beat the crap out of each other and don't just go screaming to the police. It takes women acting like the clucking hens they once used to be and policing liberal women out of the ranks. It takes wheeling and subversive dealing to get one up on the dipstick politicians and lawyers screwing everything up. It takes buy-in on the ranch: that ranch life is the best life and what is touted as "development" and "progress" is civilizational poison. You can't let the Western genre fall into the hands of those who don't have a sense about it. You have to fight through the screwed logic of liberals in order to put things back in their place. I don't know if the show will do this. I would direct everything differently. For a glimpse at that, read my book *Fire In The Pines*. I will probably do another Western book before too long. The setup of *Yellowstone* is compelling enough for tens of millions of Americans to watch the show, root for John Dutton despite his "toxic male" aggression, and give the show a high rating on many review sites. People want the ranch protected. People don't want to have to leave places like Virginia, Pennsylvania, Illinois, Oregon, or Ohio because the liberals have mucked everything up. They want to stay near their hometowns and keep the ranches going. There's no sense in everyone piling into Idaho, Montana, and Colorado just to get a fleeting taste of what once was. People want to *go home*. People aren't that happy in the Mountain West. They're tense. A lot of them are simply waiting for the dam to break so they can head back to where they came from. So long the Chinese are prevented from buying in, and the ruling regime crumbles, all these transplants will leave behind them a pockmarked mess of garbage subdivisions and loveless town homes. Soon enough, the American man will find his testicular fortitude and will once again expand *outward*. It's going to take a group strategy to pull it off. They used to make race horse movies firmly set in Kentucky's rolling hills. You'd see the wonderful vistas and the dew on the grass for the majestic horses to graze at first light. People want to *go home*. Yellowstone is not home. It's the last bastion. It will hold. The right pieces are coming together, irrespective of where Hollywood writers and Kevin Costner opt to take their TV show. The undercurrents of this show's first season are right on point with the plight of True Americans. Thank goodness they're being portrayed somewhat sympathetically for once in this age of globalist empire.

(Update: I just watched the first episode of the second season. Wow, everything is going to PC garbage. What is wrong with people? Libs destroy everything they touch.)

(Second Update: Alright, I'm seven episodes through season two. Holy cow, things are good! All you have to do is skip the scenes with the Marxist squaw. What a great show. Maybe I'll do another write-up with some more thoughts on this thing.)

(Third Update: Season three is an improvement from season two!)

The Hatred of Excellence

You can spot liberals pretty easily, especially white liberals. They have sour faces. You can see their self-hatred and their shame. The self-hatred is that they've compromised their own consciences so many times that a hardened mask forms. They cannot get back to a sense of goodness, wholeness, and decency about themselves. They are forever thrown off center and can only maintain any kind of normalcy through further self-effacement. The self-effacement accrues over time and spills out into symbolic displays of self-hatred such as: tattoos, weird piercings or earrings, extreme hair-dos, strange pantsuits on women, bleached blonde short hair on women, stooping postures issues in men, obesity, overdone makeup, odd cackles and laughs, stuttering, forgetfulness, and other such displays. What liberals represent is getting so bad and so overt that they all are starting to look like comic book villains, but a dystopian, out of shape version raised on a diet of factory food.

The shame component is that they *know* they survive by stealing from others. They are verbal manipulators, though in recent times they're turning more and more to violence. Liberals have all been exposed to arguments for liberty, they have simply sneered or absconded in the face of better ideas. They have personal hang-ups, addictions, grandiosity, debts, or ugly pasts to deal with. Public education and the media do such a number on human beings. They fill people with terrible ideas that lead them to compromise their personal integrities at young ages, ages so young that recovery is made nearly impossible. That is what the surgeries and hormone experiments are a manifestation of. Liberal "charity", as depicted in television, was always about depriving oneself and one's family for the benefit of others less capable. Jobs creation has never been depicted as a charitable act but one of greed. The liberal depiction of a classical education has always been about paralyzing one's own good judgment for the benefit of bankers, while posturing as some kind champion of the people. Liberals always encourage early sexual experimentation for the sake of pleasure as a way of destroying people's innocence and enslaving them to carnal desire. Liberals delight more from younger victims to worldly pleasures. Liberal storytelling was always about women unrealistically besting men. Now they use cinema to blow out people's reasoning ability, using memetic CGI imagery. They carefully insert symbolic programming intended to make people sympathetic to the aims and goals of One World Government. It has become so easy and streamlined for them that their moneymen simply choose the most effed up looking "director" they can find and give him a massive budget to put whatever he'd like on screen, knowing he will work hard to earn his keep and hypnotize and harm as many children as possible. The blockbusters of today are directed by people who have had credible allegations of pedophilia lodged against them. The Machine *prefers* this.

All of this ugly thinking displays itself in a person's appearance and in their countenance. Some of the more self-conscious liberals are aware at just how repulsive they are to natural people and so they try to throw people off the scent. They hike up their breasts to a comical degree. They get injections in their butts. They wear whatever the Hollywood beauty moguls are hawking. They wear expensive clothing. They have their stomachs stapled. Breast augmentations to them are a dime a dozen. They get teeth whitening. They put goofy, simplistic art in gigantic frames on their walls. They speak rapidly. They surround themselves with displays of consumerist fantasy.

The most ruthless and left-leaning liberals don't hide anything at all, which is refreshing to some extent. They *let* you see how ugly they've become. They take pleasure in your disgust and rub it in your face. This breed of liberal is accurately described as Marxist and usually their ranks are populated less by the "white liberal", though this is changing. The LGBTQ contingent of the liberals has a lot of people like this and you can spot them by their neon hair colors, armpit hair, and heavy-set cheeks. The "body positivity" movement simply normalizes open aggression against others. Obesity is the signal to others that a person is a burden upon resources. They consume too many resources and now it is *okay* for them to do so.

You have to watch out for liberals. They hate everything that is excellent and they control most of the major metropolitan areas and government institutions in the United States. It is easy to spot them, if you practice enough. Empathize with them and sense their self-loathing, envy, wrath, shame, and spiritual hideousness. They have "tells" now. They used to have to hide everything and take on the appearance of cowboys, pioneers, settlers, small businessmen, homebodies, and calendar girls. They have reengineered existence for themselves so that now they can more embody their archetypical roles as perverts, molesters, thieves, layabouts, street criminals, bankers (hahaha), demons, child murderers, human torture scientists, prostitutes, and degenerates. Yet, they do not have final victory so keep an eye out on how despite being emboldened to display these roles, they *still* have to use verbal manipulation to get good men to give up their stations. Think of a fortress that is overrun but still holding portions of the inner core where the women and children are being protected. Yes, the attacking force is busting through and picking off women and children and things are dire but the full sweep has not yet taken place. The men are holding off the invader goblins sufficiently enough that though diseases and starvation are sweeping through the protected people, the goblins still have to come at night and whisper through the broken windows. There is *still* an element of seduction to everything the goblins have to do. The slave camps may be fully constructed but they remain relatively unpopulated. Do not underestimate the strength of the men that remain. It is a trick of the goblins to sow doubt. They lie and lie, convincing otherwise good men to promise a collapse and that things will be better thereafter. Give up your arms and though tens of millions will die, somehow there will still be a rainbow afterwards. This is seduction. This is defeatism dressed up as noble withdrawal. These formerly strong men who now work from within are inclined to overplay their kindness and tenderness since after all, they are not engaged in goblin slaying anymore. Liberals take on all shapes and forms. There are also formerly strong men who get goblin-infected and try to peel off contingents of men to die needlessly. These perverted types *glow in the dark*. They lead bands off men out of the fortress and into the darkness, where their glow attracts the murderous goblins. Hopefully you get the picture. Seeing and noticing is highly valuable to both sides. The goblins have peeled off a lot of talent through the intelligence services and the elite universities. The fortress protectors, who used to go out and conquer lands to add to the kingdom, only have talent by virtue of good breeding, Christianity, homeschooling, and a few rare souls who benefitted from none of these but still somehow found their way out from the cold. The goblins hate this last type in particular because these reformed types have special knowledge of enemy tactics.

If you can see how someone is turned against their own kind, humankind, you can spread the alarm and help others to be adequately on the defense when the inevitable attacks come. But a defensive strategy is no longer enough. Like in *Lord of The Rings: Two Towers*, it is getting to the point where you have to "ride out and meet them". The last charge, which should be successful because the enemy literally has no defensive tactics other than to hide underground and fire off orbital canons, is still pawing about to find consensus in the defenders. Everyone wants to be "the King" and few still want to get behind the actual King: Jesus Christ. In the *LOTR* movie, there's easy consensus on "ride out and meet them" when in reality, it is a painstakingly long process.

There's also the simple fact that liberals are just uglier than conservatives. Surveys bear this out. You can look with your own eyes. Even the liberal celebrities are ugly, especially the globalist ones. They're hideous! It had to be said. It's the corrupting effect their criminality has on them and yes, lying to people is criminal. You used to be able to sue people for screwing with your hard-won reputation. There's legions of criminals besmirching America's reputation.

Tenacity in Business

There's a difference between being *tough* in business and screwing people. Certain people newer to America don't understand this because it's absolutely cutthroat where they come from. You have to bear in mind that most of the rest of the planet lives in abject squalor where criminal cartels run everything and there's no joy or hope. There is simply unending misery and the horizon dims and dims because IQ is dropping and nobody is even aware enough to realize it. To do business in these places, you have to criminalize your enterprise or everything will be taken from you by the local magistrate. America is becoming this way, unfortunately, hence the words earlier on the show *Yellowstone*. Conservatives are realizing they're going to have to get *tough* in their dealings, as a condition of the worsening situation in America. There is no miracle cure. Trump isn't going to ride in and save the day. He keeps endorsing absolute knot-heads that hate his guts. DeSantis might make some noise but he might stay in Florida. He doesn't want to get put in the back of an open-air limo, so to speak. There might be hot wars with Russia, Iran, and maybe China. The troops are being pulled out of Afghanistan to be sicked on the American people. Contrived gasoline shortages are popping up out of thin air. And somehow, through all this, you have to feed yourself and turn a buck.

It is not going to be easy to make a living for yourself. I have already talked about upskilling, a thousand times. I have talked about the seductive allure of working dishonest jobs. I'll talk only a bit about being tough in business cause there's other stuff I want to get to. You need to build up stuff that people want. These can be digital assets. They can be physical. You've got to stockpile these things, like the Money Masters have, and then you make appeals to people to do stuff for you (job creation) or you negotiate with people who want the stuff you have. When you do this, you want to be firm but fair. You *always* want to favor moral people in your dealings. Don't do deals with bureaucrats, journalists, real estate developers, unions, illegals, illegal sympathizers, cosmopolitans, or corporations. They will use a single transaction with you to get a foothold into your business dealings to then, down the road, steal what is yours. Marketing is immoral. It always has been. When you market, you have to lower your standards. When you lower your standards low enough, you will have to normalize dealings with criminals. This is why big box stores have cages and locked cases around certain items. They have "loss prevention officers" to stop looters. These are compromised enterprises and just as they tolerate criminality in order to operate in a public-facing manner, so do they steal from the American people on the back end by donating primarily to Democrat politicians. Marketing, and especially advertising itself, puts your stuff out there to be messed with by the envious. I understand that to even get up off the ground in today's business environment, you will probably have to run an ad or sell yourself a bit in an interview. It's a near guarantee. I am talking about an *ideal* to try and stick to as you scale up and improve your status. We live in a messed-up Attention Economy helmed by Millennials and broken brain Gen-Xers who are butt slaves to bankers. Don't like it? Doesn't change that it's true. Go on a single airline flight and tell me what the "marketing" consists of. It's all evil. But I digress.

When you're tough in business, you understand that what you have is worth something to you and you *could* work it to yield for you but you're wanting to put it out there so someone else will do something with it. Honest business is a form of generosity. You don't need a bunch of welfare or even charities if you have an honest business environment. The only way to have an honest business environment is for nobody to transact with corporations, block out international finance for the kabillionth time in world history, and to jail anyone who wants to increase government spending – *especially* when they are advocating for income taxes instead of tariffs. Tariffs are *OK* but you want that money poured into measures that prevent immigration into your country, not the pockets of fat cat party bosses. Being tough in business means overcoming objections, making counteroffers, not revealing weakness or a diminished position, pointing out to people when they're unreasonable in a way that doesn't weaken you or them (which is tricky!), and ensuring that turdbirds *never ever* get a seat at the table. To ensure excellence in business, you have to keep leftist ideologues from having authority – even if they're *fantastic* money earners. A lot of people don't understand this. The GOP is run by business people who love capitalism, are generally overweight, and make it a point of pride and distinction in their companies that there is *zero* discrimination going on in terms of a person's political orientation. The left doesn't think this way. They deliberately exclude anyone who wants less government in the world. People have to remember that discrimination laws, which only ever work one way, were literally invented by greedy neurotic types in the past century to give them a performative advantage. I am not saying do anything illegal. I am talking about *ideals* when I say that ideologues should never be promoted to a position of influence. This is a book about ideals. Period. Got it? I have Japzilla punching King Kang in the balls. This is entertainment. We're talking about how things have come to be the way they are and how they will reliably become, given those facts. I am not saying "go out and vote for this candidate" or "go and break this law". Obey the law!

These people that run the GOP have made *ideals* out of Civil Rights and all manner of other nonsense that was passed into law in the 20th Century. They have an extremely short memory but they play the patriot and get appearances on Fox News and such. They sell you mugs, highlight their black friends via tokenism, and sprout coffee grounds companies in their wake like pigeons pooping on park benches. They don't remember what America *actually* used to be like. They're business pigeons! Or parrots. Blah-blah-blah we love cheeseburgers and consumer spending to our individual preferences. That's individualism and the American way! Don't get me started on these people. You can't learn how to get real tough, with these people as your mentors. They all cuck out on the most important issue: personnel. Personnel is policy. In an ideal world, you can't hire evil people with garbage voting patterns to earn a portion of what value you add to the world.

The *real* patriots have essentially turned to self-employed entrepreneurship, small-scale enterprise where they can't be forced by some wine guzzling pinko from Seattle to bring Somali terrorists into the kitchen to flip burgers. The left has figured out that this is where *real* patriots have retreated to and it pisses them off badly because there's little left for them to do besides messing with zoning laws and then moving on to outright aggression. You want to try and find these guys and help them out. They're hard to track down, with good reason. If you're a young, based dude, you will want to be excellent every day until one of these guys makes himself known to you and then you protect him with all your might from subterfuge while adding value to his enterprise. This is how you make an honest living and the entire organized government apparatus of the world is set against you, aside from a few places like Oklahoma, Texas, Florida, Iowa, Idaho, Missouri, Arkansas, Poland, Hungary, Slovakia, Singapore, and maybe Australia but it's been a few years since I've been there. The best kept secret of the world has leaked out and it's your job to do what is right by putting stock in the right people. People are irreplaceable. Ideas can be killed if you kill the people who hold those ideas, duh. How have people on the right and on the anti-government side of things have not figured this out yet or at least publicly acknowledged it? Take care of and augment the good people, who pass their personalities and values down to their children. Ally yourself with them and do legal but *tough* business.

The evil people can't stop this because it's all voluntary and an objective good for the world. All they can do is smear me and censor me. The message is already out. Every copy of this book could be burned and its digital existence deleted forever and the message is still out. Just make sure those who carry the message aren't snuffed out. As long as we have lungs to breathe and mouths to speak, the message will get out and it will spread quickly. They can't put 100 or 200 million people in solitary confinement. They tried! Last year! And it didn't work. The human spirit is too prevailing. It is too enduring. They won't even be able to genetically engineer it out of us but that's the latest thing they're into, the evil ones. It won't work even if they molest all of the conservative children. It will only work if they do a total genocide and they won't be able to do it. Their most prominent, wealthy leaders have acknowledged that they can't by saying that "nationalism is a permanent fixture, whether we like it or not". The more honest, transparent thing to have said would have been, "Gee, we can't genocide them all! That's inconvenient but nonetheless, we've only been set back a few decades." Let's set them back even more. Let's run them out of every nook and cranny they've dug into. We can only do that if we get *tough* in business and starting doing the right thing.

The Misguided Universalizing Tendency of Conservatives

Liberals are made out to be people that have good intentions for the world but they're just misguided on how to get there. This is the political answer. Framing liberals this way *does* allow them wiggle room to realize that their proposed solutions are wrong but it does not confront them with their own worship of death. Pro-life activists do this effectively by going to college campuses and displaying banners of aborted babies. There is a *butchery* involved in what the liberal proposes. Everyone should be equal, therefore unequal people have to either be subsidized or stolen from against their will. Stealing from people is okay because "colonialism" a long time ago or slavery an even longer time ago. Liberals know that stealing is wrong but they don't care because they think the ends justify the means. We could be more forgiving of liberals in generations past because there was so much abundance and so little immediate feedback on consequences for evil policies but that forgiveness is wearing thin as American cities burn every single night. Nowadays there are liberal hate mobs bussing from one place to another, harassing people and destroying lives, while funded by the richest liberals who would happily put down their feral dogs the moment the dogs turned. Liberals have totally mobilized the true nature of their political schemes. They are soon going to blot out the sky. The feedback is shorter and shorter. With a stroke of the pen, a senile liberal can wipe tens of thousands of jobs off the board and liberals don't even care. They're craven. They don't celebrate anything anymore, not even homosexuality. They just kill, consume, and attack without even pausing to tout their supposed victories. They used to preen about like they'd won a debate on the ideas whenever they got significant legislation passed. Now they don't even care. They're juiced-out power addicts with shot veins. Getting liberals to see this about themselves means putting a mirror in front of them. They hate what they see and lie, saying it's the conservative who is this hideous apparition. The lying runs at least three levels deep, as mentioned earlier. Putting that much work into people who are in a perpetual trantrum is simply becoming too much work for people in their personal lives. Online platformers and talking heads were picking up the slack for a while but they've been run into ghettos.

Conservatives have this terrible habit going on where they universalize everything, irrespective of reciprocity. Equality under the law is their ideal, more or less, and they don't put themselves in the shoes of the Founders at all whatsoever when making their assessments. Clearly, the Founders didn't mean, "Invite Barbary pirates into the country to the tune of millions and then try to share a legal system with them." In order to not be painted as "racists" by the liberal media, who paints away anyway, these horrible cowards and misguided non-thinkers try to do tokenism or bellyache that they're the least racist person ever. This doesn't work.

The best conservatives are figuring out that you can't just open your coffers to stupid, aggressive people who will only ever steal from you and never exchange at a fair rate. Some libertarians, non-definables, and others have also started figuring this out but they're supremely cagey about naming actual causes to things and would rather just navigate consequences more efficiently. You can't assume that everyone is just going to "figure it out" like you will, as a part of your heritage. Craigslist transactions don't exactly go smoothly in enriched areas, so to speak. In fact, they're an easy way to catch a beating in those places. Or to have your place prospected by burglars. The trust is so stupidly low in parts of America. Conservatives are slow to realize this. They think if they just speak out against socialism that they've done their part. The job requires more than that. You cannot reasonably be a conservative leader in 2021 with talking points from 2013. The responsibility is mounting, every single day. While censorship is difficult to contend with and the job pays mostly only future dividends, it's a worthwhile job to take up. The reward is a clean conscience, less dysfunction in the personality, and a *legal* path forward for the nation's institutions to reflect morality and goodness back to the people. Some, who stipulate constantly that they in fact are not cynical, say that there is no path forward and that insufficient people have learned the lessons of history on totalitarianism. While this may even be true, and therefore does not need stipulations attached, it doesn't change that by bringing truth to people about the most important issues you open up the world to more survivors beyond the collapse. If a collapse is assured, then you can focus on things differently. You can enjoy your life more while still making a critical difference. And then there is also the elitist sentiment that you ought not to care about people's lives more than they care about their own. This is sane and I sympathize to a large extent. Yet, this is a conceptualization that only intellectually mature people arrive to. There are still so many people in the world who don't even know to think this way. Every young man with his life's work still *ahead* of him will want to bring this level of sanity to whoever they can, in the struggle to climb upwards and stake a place in this world for the next generation.

Conservatives are suckers for suckers. They want to rehab everybody and have become corpulent, ugly, and lazy themselves. You have to watch for your standards to erode over time. Unless you're conceptually fully mature *before* you hit peak IQ, you basically are caught in this battle by your late 20's of having a slowly dropping IQ in a poisoned natural environment bumping up against your thinking continuing to mature over time. Unless you do the work *early* in your development, you're basically unaware sometimes of how you backslide because you never hit peak maturity and IQ at the same time. Men are starting to understand this with women. They understand that a woman over the age of 21 is a *project* and that investment is a riskier and riskier proposition. There's a similar thing going on with men, too. The age is a *wee* bit higher but not by much. *Maybe* two years. And guys don't want to face that. They don't want to face the dual edged razor tip of the mountaintop thing that happens where you can fall off either side because of false intellectual certainty on the one hand or cruddy emotional underdevelopment on the other – all while attempting to scale higher and higher. You have to do the work early. You have to stay sober and clean. There's no way around it. People don't want to do this and so they focus on figures to rehab, out in the world. These are reflections of their inner selves but at a distance, so the discomfort doesn't get too great. The West was convinced to make a wrong turn at a certain point. Yeah, people like ugly. They watch TV where people act like dog crap brutes to each other and then nary blink an eye when they're ugly with the people in their own lives. And then you add 100 million outsiders into the milieu and it's no wonder America is *rapidly* disintegrating. Our cultural introspection was on a whole nother level before television. Who wants to keep that going? Guys get a few political principles down and they think they're prepared to save the entire civilization. They watch some street person's livestream and they think, "I'm making a difference!" They watch harmless foreign intelligence services agents dawdle around Washington D.C. and think they're in the real juice. They read some esoteric B.S. book that never meant anything and think they're being *really intellectual*. It's a ghetto. The near entirety of modern conservative thought is a hateful, mediocre, retarded ghetto. And the LARPers who somewhat realize this don't make it any easier for the real artists. They haven't lived well. They haven't lived and bled as real human beings. No amount of tastefully collected art from antiquity will change that. They're turds, uninspired turds who hide behind dogma. All that IQ amounting to nothing. It's a crime. It's a crime against humanity but who is left to dole out the consequences? It's just rabid hordes everywhere.

It's all panic and decay with a few money grubbers leaning on top of it all. There's more, too.

I had one of these LARPers attack me. He did a relatively high-level attack. Enough to throw me off for a second until I figured it out. He's so crusty, though. His brain is filled with, well... I won't say. I won't give away too many tricks. He's crusty, we'll leave it at that. And I hadn't encountered quite the variation of attack he did on me, so kudos to him. It was so strange to be around him because he pretended to not notice that I was noticing everything he did. I was open about what I was doing because I have no need to hide my curiosity around those whom I presume are my friends. He was not open about what he was doing. He was gathering what he could on me to try and use it against me later, which I see now is what he thought I was doing. But I'm not into that. I am into something else that I won't say. I'm into beauty, is the extent of what I will say. This is a person that is widely respected and even venerated. Yet he stepped to me with this hideous assault. He tried to kill my spirit. It didn't work. He used thousands and thousands of hours of *learned* scholasticism against me, honed to a fine point edge, and it did not work. He has felled so many others. High IQ people I've known, too. Wealthy people. All manner of high achievers. But it fell flat and it just made me annoyed. Shoo, fly. They do this stuff. Here I am, doing what I'm doing in the distant background, and now and then they try to do this stuff. I won't say more. There's too many sociopaths out there thirsting for the other bits.

The bigotry of ideologues is coming back and *not* in the way that supposed enlightened centrists posit. It's different and it's on all sides. It's the relinquishment of consciousness made into a cult. The world has a hankering for death because stupid people have been allowed to make the decisions. There are conmen, *especially* on the conservative side, that have come out to roost and feast on the splayed guts of people ripping themselves apart. We have a long way to go. We all have to deal with the child abusers, first. All of us, together. No shortcuts!

Cattle Lines

People find themselves more and more often in line for "essential services". Look at the videos of people forming huge lines to get jabbed by the government. They're an accurate reflection of the mindset of people in huge liberal population centers but they are also probably broadly distributed to lower morale. There has been a resistance wall that has been hit in the United States. Thousands of appointments for people to get jabbed are going unfilled. Experts predict that the USA will only hit 60% injection coverage, which is 10% short of what is supposedly needed for herd immunity. The reports of terrible, deadly, life-altering injures from these things are rolling in. Where there's the most free-speech legally enshrined, the people fair the best. Imagine that.

You look at these videos and you realize these people are zombies. They just do what they're told. They comply with mandates. A not insignificant proportion of these people standing in line is made up of newcomers to the West. Things are so bad in their homelands that they figure being openly treated like a cow before slaughter is preferable to going back home and scratching out a living. Until currency collapse, this will remain true. But *after* currency collapse, things are going to get buck wild. This book was supposed to be lighter and funnier but this is the way the writing has sloped. Maybe I have to get these things out before we can get back to the funny stuff.

The zombie movies are accurate reflections of a psychological war that is playing out. There are no assurances anymore as we live in a post-ethical age. If you find yourself standing in a line with other vulnerable people, you're in deep dookie. You don't want to find yourself in that situation. Perhaps you already have. This is why I am not interested in flying anymore. It's of no concern to me. I have no need to visit the other states, especially ones far away, unless I am part of some escape caravan headed down to Mexico or something. America has lost its allure. Why visit Connecticut or Delaware? They're utter hellholes. Why visit California? I don't want to die. The only place I want to visit is Florida. I'd fly to Florida. This is not to disparage people's choices about where they live in America. I love *all* of America. I have been to over 2/3rds of all of the states, including Alaska. I enjoyed the time that I spent in deep blue Virginia. Massachusetts has its charm, and so forth. It is simply to say that America is deeply, deeply ill right now and airline travel is a tremendous liability. Half of the US states are near no-go zones. They're trying to make mask mandates *permanent* in my home state of Oregon. You are most likely to find yourself standing in a huge line waiting for stuff, if you're in one of these places. Hell, you're *highly* likely to be doing that in Texas, Florida, or even a place like suburban Montana. If you ever find yourself in that bind of waiting in a huge line with hungry people, rethink your life. Many of us had to do this when the fake pandemic first struck and everyone took to

Costco to wait in line for toilet paper. These things will happen *on the regular* soon enough. Contractors wait on lumber loads to come in to Home Depot and Lowes. Meat prices creep up, month after month. Your electric bill keeps going up, despite you using less. Shortages pop up, here and there. Get as sustainable as you can, as fast as you can. We should have never relied on factory farming in the first place, even absent the massive immigrant influx. The dairy and produce lobbies of America have had as much a hand in its demise as any of the other special interest groups.

Voluntary association is going out the window with all this medical tyranny. It will be a sign of luxury to be able to be apart from other people. To go out and mingle and such used to be considered a luxury. Now it is the opposite. Just look and see what is happening in Canada or Germany. People are getting dragged from their homes and put in camps! This is no hyperbole. Yet, the tyrannical politicians enacting all of this are left unmolested. They wear a mask when they like and that's all. Even celebrities have to do rituals where they appease their Luciferian order. Even the military commanders are made to wear high heels, as men, and all other manner of self-abasement. The politicians, bankers, and Big Tech freakazoids get away the cleanest. You're just pond scum. You're a mouse. You're nothing to these lizard overlords. They'll devour you and your children for stepping out of line. Those big lines into Walmart and such have already been idly patrolled by police. They'll be patrolled by military. It's only a matter of time. It's going to get a lot worse before it gets better. People need to learn to look this fact in the eye. You can always work your best to mitigate consequences and fight back against evil but the undercurrent is obvious.

I make outsized *legal* moves in the face of this, most of it social. People are confused and don't know their role. They don't hardly do what needs to be done. They think conversations won't make a difference. They don't think to make social assurances or to store up credit with others. They are unsure of the value of telling people the truth. They think outsized requests or expectations are undue and oppressive. Your own liberation is *somewhat* within your grasp, if you'd just talk and think it through. Survival contorts and stretches us out. People don't like this. They think they can go on like everything was before. They think they'll get to raise their two children, one boy one girl, going to the park and "putting them through school". The entire planet is poisoned by xenoestrogens, chemtrails, jab side effects that radiate outward to the unjabbed, electro-magnetic frequencies, and by the horrific social chain reactions that permeate from ritual child sacrifice by the ultra-elite. People sit there on their couches, thinking that business-as-usual is just how it's going to go. Techies think they're always going to have tech work to do. Consoomers think there will always be boxed food for them. Liberals think that whitey is always going to take it. Stoners think there will always be stuff to trip out on. This world is going to be rather severe on the complacent, lazy, and unintelligent. Variations on the theme. You're supposed to become something outsized. You're supposed to be epic in your own life. People don't want to do it. They keep pointing me to mediocrities, saying how blown their minds are. Parasites circle me and the ones I love. The self-promotion in a dying civilization is only hushed by starvation, actual literal starvation. I don't need that. Leave me out of it. You better bring value if you come around. Not grandiosity. Real value. Most just don't have it. Their mediocre brains are filled with puke media and mediocre, uninspired whiners. It has to be said! It's a clawing that is happening. The lost souls falling into the gaping abyss, clawing upwards in order to not sink down forever. Who has gold in their bodies? Who will give from the heart anymore? People had such dim childhoods. No gold to give. The facsimile of it is rearing up. People "returning to tradition". It's awkward cause you're not supposed to say anything critical. We're supposed to *overcome*, not sperg inwardly. Too many excuses people put up. They all know better, don't they? Everyone's become such an armchair expert. Leave me out of it. What a joyless racket.

If you haven't been in a long line of needy people, good! If it's been a while, good as well! If it's only been a little bit, sense the danger. And even if you never have been in one of these lines, consider that maybe you still are in the line – you just can't perceive it. Perhaps, anyway. People have their blind spots. Are we allowed to say that? Is that "tradition"? The lines will eat you up. It is a horror being visited upon the world. People break and turn away. They shut me out. I pushed too hard. I have *this* bad intention or *that* bad intention. I should just play video games and be less self-serious. It'll blow over. Monasteries, nunneries, and cathedrals are demoed every week but somehow, it'll blow over. Where are the real human beings? Where is your deep, inner balance? Remember the waves of the ocean? Remember the sense of life from not so long ago? Remember the expansivity? Many voices coming together in harmony for divine beauty. This would bring us to our knees. It was everywhere. It animated all things. Now there's plastic everywhere. Everywhere on my land. I don't produce any of it. It simply blows in on the wind. My neighbors all have decent voting records. They're some of the better ones in the world. The plastic bits they churn out are everywhere. I used to pick this stuff up. I don't know if I can anymore. It poisons me every time I touch it. Do I keep gloves on me just so I can walk around in this physical world? The plastic becomes more and more toxic, too. It's not like trash picking from twenty years ago. This isn't some green cry for mercy. It's how the world is. You're not supposed to talk about your direct experience. It is bad. You will be harangued by high IQ people who effin' hate your guts or mid IQ people who purity test you. Do you raise your children to pick up trash or do you raise them to leave it be? It's hard to say anymore.

Shot Down

I stopped by to see my buddy the other day. Yes, I drove my truck. I had the country station on that only plays 70s, 80s, and 90s hits. Sometimes they play modern stuff but only Chris Stapleton or Morgan Wallen, the good stuff. Country music is making a comeback! And no, they don't play that Darius Rucker BS. He sucks. He should have kept being Hootie. The more of an off-hour you get this station going, the more obscure the songs are and the deeper it hits. Nothing like going into the B-side deep cuts on some well-made album from the 80s. When I pulled in to my buddy's place, Mark Chesnutt was playing. Those Texas players have something special in them.

I got to talking to my buddy and everything out of his mouth wasn't him at all. It was somebody else. It was like he was rehearsed. He had an answer for everything. It was his family members talking through him, like he'd been coached. Everything was about safety, staying close to family, being humble and all this other stuff that well anticipated my risk-taking bent. It was like his soul was under storm shutters or something. I couldn't get through to the guy. The conversation was over before it even started. We just sat there for twenty minutes on some hay bales he was bucking and then it was time to go. He didn't listen to me. He was nervous, like it was a job interview that wasn't going to go his way. I wanted him to join the outfit. He just wanted to rehash his family's memories on their behalf. His grandmother hovered nearby for a moment, obviously trying to listen in on our conversation. Really, buddy? This is how much they control you? You're like a puppet for them and they've trained you to love it. We've got to get out of here! There's danger, you've said it yourself. You say you're surrounded by the enemy out there but maybe the people living here on this property with you aren't so friendly themselves.

He lives in the mental world where this kind of thought just isn't permitted. It's a state of primitiveness this guy's family has kept him in. Family is the end all, be all! How dare I point this out? This is some kind of leftist seduction, they'll intimate. My buddy is a grown person. He can choose for himself, I say. It doesn't matter and it especially wouldn't matter if I was a woman making a similar proposition: come join the outfit for a bit. They'd try to take that woman and crash and burn her in this place. Keep her here, keep her stuck. If she complains, that's feminism. Some people have bright spirits and they have to be snuffed out. It's good for the family! Don't change, don't grow. Don't innovate, don't adventure. Stay stuck here, rehashing memories that are convenient only in one direction. For a second there, I thought his grandma had a pitchfork. I see, I'm the enemy. I'm not to be trusted because I'm different than the orthodoxy. Repeat the orthodoxy at all costs, even if it has been well accounted for by the enemy. People are desperate for nothing to change. They hack down anybody who innovates. How is this farm supposed to survive? How is this county going to make it?

I hopped in my truck and drove back out the muddy drive, waving my hand out the open window. I could see in the rearview he wanted to come along and join the outfit. I could see it in his body language. People cast such aspersions on this cowpoke. Everywhere he goes, the doors slam shut. Try something different. The world is burning. Nobody wants to hear it. Back on the highway I went. I watched the one elk herd in the area slowly walk along the tree line. I entered into where the town is aggressively expanding. BS, cookie cutter houses tapping in to an aquifer they don't deserve. Then I was in town proper. I thought about how that place back there was surrounded by enemies. He said it as much, himself. You can't believe it until you're there. Then you see as you peer out that his enemies have rifles pointed in to his parents' place. You wouldn't think this could happen in America but here we are. Their security cameras go off nearly every night. I'm saying: come join the outfit. We're in the mountains. He wouldn't hear it. The storm of aspersions a paranoid group of people will cast on the outsider who talks sense…it's like a version of tall poppy syndrome. Buddy, your soul is going to starve.

Bad Pairings

Bad pairings happen all the time. Selection has gone to hell. Promiscuity covers up early mistakes and then people find themselves feeling *stranded* long after the fact. Despite the upside-down nature of our current CIA world, it is still more difficult for a woman who is stranded than a man. Men are so completely and totally expendable at this point that even with feminism arming women to the teeth, a man can more or less slip away unscathed. Not the same for a woman, especially if she's slept with the man. I have less sympathy for women who are stranded, because they have their pick of the litter. There are so many thirsty dudes sitting around on the apps, hoping for romantic rescue…and a few of them are hoping to enter the gene pool. Plus, you have to factor in the entire Third World since the dating market has become globalized. But I still have sympathy for women who are stranded. It's a massive problem, for some reason. A lot of it can be explained away by acknowledging that feminism puts unrealistic expectations in women's heads but not all of it. There's this significant wedge of the woman pie where a woman, because of her access to the Internet, has special knowledge that a man may not or chooses to remain in ignorance of. The ghey Boomer version of this is the woman who is a classical liberal in her head and has had some degree of financial success. She therefore feels "enlightened" or "empowered" and her life retains a sense of glamour. It's a bad corollary but it's the closest one that comes to mind. Women have bitten the forbidden fruit of knowledge via social media but remain in the un-fathered state that they are, so cruddy men get in when they otherwise wouldn't be able. And the dissatisfaction persists. What to do about this?

Remediating the man on a broad scale is one viable solution. I focus a lot of my energies into this. This does not resolve the *stranded* aspect of a bad pairing. A man's motivation to remediate once he has a woman bagged is a lot lower, especially to do it on the woman's behalf. She was foolish enough to get with him in the first place. He has emotional leverage! The more cunning men or the losers who have their backs to the wall are the ones who use this emotional leverage but let's be real, most relationships are grey and dissociated and nobody makes these considerations. Most of this stuff remains unconscious. Even if a person has a Machiavellian personality, he's still doing it out of a tendency rather than some conscious plan. Women are extremely easy to manipulate when they're un-fathered or under-fathered and it's a race to see who gets first contact. Social media made first contact. Everyone else comes after the fact. A lot of this stranding, bad pairing, and general misery in human romantic relationships would be resolved by banning women from the Internet entirely. It's just a logical sequence of reasoning, any opinions of mine aside. Most men are *not* interested in making their women excellent. Most men are dissociated diaper babies who want sexual relief and the woman to be the breadwinner so he can stay in the apartment and be on the Internet. I have a little bit of sympathy for these guys. No more brother wars! However, if you're not a part of the solution, you're a part of the problem – especially if you're going around voting for globalism.

When on a broad scale you remediate the man with lessons on masculinity, you better prepare them to face the world and to face down the evil in women. It's kind of evil and manipulative for a woman to fall *stranded* to a man and then cry for help after the fact. It's learned helplessness. It's passive aggressive. It's a form of dishonesty. But you also understand it since people can't very well help *when* they get redpilled. Waking up one day and realizing you're *stranded* happens to the best of us. In fact, it's kind of the only way it happens. Let's face it, nobody talks to each other substantively anymore. Good ideas filter through to us mainly through Internet searches and random things popping up on the timeline. You can't help the timing of this, only hasten it to some extent. I choose to help the man first. Every single man that I have reached through my offerings is *much better* equipped to deal with pairing excellence. Men appear to have more agency, a *lot* more agency. You have to work things through them first. A cry for help from a woman who's paired with a man who isn't in the fraternity or who is just barely keeping one toe in it is such a mess and so far late into the game. There are a few options but none of them are favorable. It's dirty work. Priests and pastors before feminism used to have to do it. The single moms used to be administered to by the clergy. There was a way of socially shaping things so that women wouldn't fall into these traps. The failures of the father could be mitigated. The overreach of manipulative, invasive mothers was tempered by Christianity. Everything ran so much more smoothly! I miss it!

I have made a video or two on Men/Women Who Settle that have resonated a lot with people. This was back before I was censored by the regime. These were basic primers on the subject. Settling is real. Men and women used to compete with their own sexes, in person. Think of it. There was a sporting, sorting component to dating. The isolation that social media has bred, exacerbated by tyrannical government lockdowns, has completely obliterated the lived experience of *competition* in dating. You had to be better than the next guy. You had to be ambitious as a woman and aim high. There were all these social cues you just followed and things turned out more or less well for you. Dating needs a social context. It's not the Uber Eats delivery service that it has been morphed into by Big Tech. Your buddies need to vet a woman. Your group of girls needs to vet a man. They ensure good selection! We need to live our lives in social groups, not alone on the computer. True success through online dating is low. Yes, there have been countless pairings made but the *quality* has gone down. We need sock hops, lovers lane, Youth Group, pubs, honky-tonks, and other gatherings where young people, in their groups and apart from their families, can contribute to a sorting group logic. This can only happen when strong conservative men run the culture. The requirement here is exclusivity. Others, with garbage cultures and sensibilities, must be excluded. The legal trend is in the complete opposite, Satanic direction. Good luck, everyone! Speak up while you can.

If you're a single person, focus on making friends. If you're a woman, make female friends. It's not easy but don't be one of these loser women who "only has guy friends" or just hangs around her family like a love cripple. You have an imperative to have female friends. If they're difficult, so what? Everything social ever is difficult, especially with smartphones clotting everything up. Women need to wrangle difficult women. Women need to learn how to get along so they can actually look out for one another, instead of remaining annoying, cringe economic units for banksters and horny Third Worlders to exploit. Your sisterhood was liberalized and then stolen from you. You used to be so *together*. Take it back. Just don't be a cringe wignat about it. Be a reasonable human being. You're doing it for the security, not to make a statement about your identity. Single women should not be focused on fishing lonely milky boys off of social media. No, you don't have "online friends". You're just a perverted woman who can't admit it. Single women should have female friends. It's difficult! Women want to work, have apartment dogs, drink coffee, and collect online milky boys. Feminism is cancer. You have a job to do. Make friends. Restore your communal bonds. It's not some cosmopolitan, classical liberal ideal. Women used to talk to each other, you know? A lot, actually. Especially back in the Middle Ages. It wasn't Sex In The City. It was women talking. That's it. But it worked and a lot of good things came out of it. The woman who gets stranded is the woman who goes on Prickle, or whatever the dating app is called, and gets a peepee boy. The woman who has a lot of women to talk to, that aren't feminist, is the woman who is plugged in. It basically doesn't exist anymore. I'm describing a social unicorn. It can be done and I've seen extremely few instances of it. No, being friends with your boyfriend's friend's girlfriends is not the same thing. No, consulting your sisters and your mother is not the same thing. It's closer but it's still not the same thing. For some crazy reason, women still tend to give each other useful advice even if their own lives are total garbage. I can't explain it. It's beyond my powers, at the moment. It happens. Seen it with me own eyes. What a thing for a young woman to consider, that she'd talk to other women first. Older women don't have that luxury. Your fertility wall fast approaches, old gal! Get yourself a cowboy before your eggs dry up.

The same advice applies to men, too. Hunt in a pack. Make male friends first. If you're lonely, check to see if it's a loneliness borne out of a lack of male companionship. That's a thing. It's common. So many men desperately scan the dating app, finally get the girl, and are still unfulfilled despite getting their rubbies and huggies from a milky momma. Fancy that. The best fulfillment a woman can offer you is when you look each other in the eye after you've had babies. It's still not the same as having male companionship. Having a male friend for decades is a darn good deal. You're bonded in a way a woman will never offer you. You can have both, of course, but make haste. The world is falling apart. I keep fighting against this theme in the book. I woke up happy this morning. Enthused about things. But it's all stuff in my control.

The tone and theme of the book keeps defaulting back to this trepidation about the world at large.

Another question that comes up with this dating stuff is, "What if this is a world historical trend that can't be fought much anymore? What if people are past the point of breeding, for a while? What if this is lead-up and anticipation of some selective event? Whoever made it, made it." I know more daughters are born when a country is being invaded, something like this. What if this is some deeply unconscious group dynamic that is playing out and is in, some ways, a healthy response to toxins in the environment? I just always kind of assumed that fertility is preferable, no matter what. Is caring more about people's parent prospects than they care about them a productive use of time? Many questions!

He Saved Her Life and She Baked Him Cookies For It

He rode down from the foothills into town in his pickup truck. She was bored for yet another day of her life, sitting on her back lawn in a lawn chair and perusing social media. Her stupid idiot liberal parents were off at government jobs, burning away the inheritance of future generations. She was supposed to be off at college but since the lockdowns were in place and her instinctive sense told her not to take the testing that would allow her to be on campus, she was living with them for the foreseeable future. She didn't mind the arrangement because her parents were *nice*, even though a bit obsessed with watching TV when they came home from their respective jobs.

He parked his pickup truck at the curb outside her house. He got out of the cab, hopped into the bed, stood up, and hollered loudly, "Heytherebaby, I'm like a shot a whiskey and you're like a glass of wine and honey we can get on outta here before the sun goes down." This broke her social media stupor and she looked up from her phone to hear some more. He hollered, "Heyprettyhoney, why dontcha slide on over. Girl I been chasing you and it's Friday afternoon and we gotta get the money in the bank." The phone slid from her hand. She adjusted her bikini, stood from her lawn chair, and went and peeked her head over the fence gate to look at this man beckoning her.

He continued, "Girl, we're like a shot whiskey and we gotta get risky if we're gonna shake this town and go somewhere with less people like the country."

She was hypnotized. He wasn't a spectacularly handsome man. She was more attractive than him. It was the things he said that spoke to something in her. It's like he had the keys to undo all of her rotten liberal programing. It's like he had the cultural power to outcompete hip hop culture and its adherents. She did not have the words to articulate this and wouldn't for at least five years to come. Looking out on him, she felt a thrill she hadn't felt since she was in grade school and kissing boys was still uncancelled.

He hopped down from the truck and marched across the lawn, saying, "Redheadhoney we gotta get a little money. Nothing like red dirt barbeque living, I'll be a shooting guard with a Winchester loaded at the ready." He gestured for her to step back from the gate her fat dad had let fall into noticeable disrepair. She did what this interloper. He kicked down the gate full force with his cowboy boot. She felt excited all over her body and even though she'd had two sex partners and a lesbian dalliance off at college, this was the first time she'd ever felt this way. He grabbed her by her waist and slung her over his shoulder and started to whirl around to go back to his truck when a neighbor who'd seen the gate kicked down yelled from her window, "Stop! You can't just kidnap her. That's rape culture. I'm calling the police!"

The Man hollered back, "Yeahlittle sugar I need a boat. We're gonna go out on the lake and float. Been a long time since I been in love but with you girl we're gonna play baseball with a baseball glove."

The neighbor stopped picking up the phone receiver and set it down. She paused and then shut her window. The Man took his Woman and was in the front yard when her father showed up early from work in his Ford Focus.

He squeezed his corpulent liberal body out of the Focus and yelled, "Hey, where are you taking my daughter? Who are you? You're not a minority. You're not allowed, you redneck!"

"Sipping off something from a paper sack. Guess I'm still chasing you girl like a shot of something good. Uh-huh, you got what I need, let's get out of this town. Chasing that small-town vibe. Still thinkin' bout you, like tequila on my mind. Bartender let er' go and drink her nice and slow." The Man continued to carry his Woman toward his old truck parked at the curb.

The father roared, "Oh no, you don't – you white abuser! MSNBC and CNN told me about you. My daughter is to only destroy her life, not improve it with someone of her own kind. I can't let you have her, you redneck supremacist. You're responsible for slavery and you're not wearing a mask for the pandemics and your skin is not the right color." The father moved his fat legs and torso in The Man's direction. "I'm going to stop you! She will not heed the ancestral call."

He came up close to The Man and The Man turned to him and held one hand up and said, "She's like a diamond jewel and I'm smoking my Juule. She been rode but she never kicked like a mule. Get er' out in the pasture where I can look at her like a shot of whiskey." This stunned the father, as if energy particles had shot out of The Man's hand. The father began to have a heart attack and crumpled to the ground. The daughter was surprised to not feel much for her father. She mostly felt resentment at him for shackling her with student loan debt, for not shielding her from the perverts who took her innocence at college, and for only gifting her with one other sibling – who was now a porn-addicted, weed-smoking loser who moonlit sometimes as a wearer-of-black at globalist funded "protests" for extra weed money.

"Girl, you're like a glass of wine," said The Man.

"Bye-bye, loser," she said to her writhing father.

The Man placed her in the passenger side of the bench seat of his truck. He got in on his side and started up the truck. He put it into gear and the truck started to move but The Woman's mother pulled up halfway into the driveway, partly blocking the suburban street with her crossover SUV. She got out and walked over to be in front of the truck.

"Where are you taking the girl I birthed by my ninth sex partner in my 30's? Seeing her get mauled to spiritual death day in and day out by Satanic technological overlords whose existence I will never acknowledge in public is what gives me joy in this life! Honey, sweetie?" she said with innocent, hard-done-by eyes as she stood there. "You can't just leave Mommy. I need you to be around cause when your fat dad dies, I'll have to psychically drain *someone* to cover up the guilt I feel for being a stupid whore when I was young and all of the times I blasphemed Christ – who I pretend doesn't exist. Watch TV with me, please! It's only 25 to 35 more years of your pointless, liberal life. Please!"

The Woman leaned her body, which had somehow morphed into a much sexier form in the past five minutes, out of the passenger window and said, "See this here is real country and I'm a Daisy Duke. He's like a shot of whiskey and he ain't never gonna puke. He slaps me on my butt when I done a good job. I came from small-town living and I ain't no part of a mob. Just have me some babies and bake some cookies. He saved my life and we gonna make a batch of rookies."

The mother fell to her knees and screamed, "No! Why, oh why? My daughter isn't going to be subtly influenced to be a hardened lesbian anymore. She is not going to be on social media anymore where I can track her every movement and leave 'loving' but subtly abusive comments on literally everything she does. I can't guide her into drinking whole bottles of wine with me and laughing at stupid, Christ-denying TV shows. Oh, no! The horror! Think of all the v*ccines I would have convinced her to take. What a terrible loss. Now I will have to double down on my loser son and make sure he gets certain surgeries and becomes my daughter slave for life. White supremacist terrorists did this to my family. My family is ruined because of the actions of other people! I will spend all of my money from here on out on organizations that deliberately and openly call for the decimation of whiteness. Their operatives will burn Christian churches to the ground and eventually kidnap white children when there are enough undocumented immigrants in the country, causing chaos wherever their economic migrant hosts decide to go. Get out of here, you terrorists! I hate you with every fiber of my being. You're dead to me. I wish I would have aborted you like I aborted your two sisters before you! Kamala haha! Kabbalah!"

The Man almost ran her over as he revved up the truck and tore out of the neighborhood. They pulled into a wedding chapel later that day and got married. As they drove back to his cabin in the foothills, he put his hand on her thigh while they sang to country music on the radio. This act alone was enough to impregnate her with twin boys who grew up to be immigration restrictionist alphas who were broad-shouldered and high IQ.

Enjoy the book?

Help book sales by leaving it a review on Amazon and Goodreads.

Printed in Great Britain
by Amazon